BERKELEY

UNIX

A Simple and
Comprehensive
Guide

JAMES WILSON

JOHN WILEY & SONS, INC.
New York   Chichester   Brisbane   Toronto   Singapore

The author and the copyright proprietor hereby disclaim all warranties, express or implied, including but not limited to the warranty of merchantability and fitness for a particular purpose. The author and the copyright proprietor have made every reasonable effort to assure that the software programs contained in this book are accurate, but assume no responsibility for any direct, indirect, incidental or consequential damage caused or sustained while utilizing the programs.

Recognizing the importance of preserving what has been written, it is a policy of John Wiley & Sons, Inc. to have books of enduring value published in the United States printed on acid-free paper, and we exert our best efforts to that end.

ACQUISITIONS EDITOR   Bob Macek
PRODUCTION MANAGER   Katharine Rubin
PRODUCTION SUPERVISOR   Micheline Frederick
COPYEDITING SUPERVISOR   Gilda Stahl
COVER AND TEXT DESIGNER   Lee Goldstein
MANUFACTURING MANAGER   Lorraine Fumoso
MARKETING MANAGER   Susan Elbe

ISBN 0-471-61582-x (pbk)

Printed in the United States of America
Printed and bound by the Hamilton Printing Company.
10 9 8 7 6 5 4

Library of Congress Cataloging-in-Publication Data

Wilson, James, 1963–
    Berkeley Unix : a simple and comprehensive guide / James Wilson.
        p.   cm.
    Includes bibliographical references and indexes.
    ISBN 0-471-61582-X (paper)
    1. Berkeley UNIX (Computer operating system)   I. Title.
QA76.76.063W56   1991
    005.4'3—dc20   90-48896
                                                                        CIP

P R E F A C E

This textbook teaches the user and programming interface for Berkeley Unix. It was designed for students with little or no knowledge of Unix and will teach them to

1. Use the Unix shell interface.
2. Program in the shell programming language.
3. Use the Unix programming interface when writing C programs.

This book is divided into three sections. The first section describes the Unix commands and the user interface. The second part describes C shell and Bourne shell programming (with a heavy emphasis on C shell programming). The last part describes the Unix programming interface for the C programming language.

I have strived for accuracy in the programming examples in this book. Every example was tested before its use. I consider all program examples in this book as public domain, provided that they are appropriately cited and not resold for profit. If you have any comments about the book, please contact me at

Bayshore Computing
2188 Ralmar Ave.
East Palo Alto, CA 94303

ABOUT THE AUTHOR

JAMES WILSON was a former lecturer at Stanford University. This book is based on the material he developed while teaching the "Introduction to Unix and C" class at Stanford University.

ACKNOWLEDGMENTS

Numerous people helped develop this book. Its production would not have been possible without their thoughtful criticisms and reviews; their suggestions had a large impact on the content and emphasis of this book.

Prof. Charles E. Frank
Northern Kentucky University

Prof. Oliver Grillmeyer
University of California–Berkeley

Prof. Evan L. Ivie
Brigham Young University

Prof. Steven Stepanek
CSU Northridge

Patricia Maples
Palo Alto, CA

I would also like to thank numerous Stanford University students for their assistance in improving the lecture notes that eventually became this book. I would especially like to thank two of my teaching assistants, Jaime Montemayor and John Walker, for their help.

Most of all, I would like to thank Earl Tondreau for encouraging me to convert my class notes into a textbook.

C O N T E N T S

v

INTRODUCTION

The UNIX* Operating System started as a result of the MULTICS project. MULTICS was a joint venture between General Electric, AT&T Bell Laboratories, and MIT to create an operating system on a GE 645 computer. MULTICS stood for "**MULT**iplexed **I**nformation and **C**omputing **S**ystem." It contributed greatly to research and understanding of the operating system concept of capabilities, but in practice it was slow and very expensive to use.

Some of the people from the MULTICS project at Bell Laboratories created UNIX. Ken Thompson, in his desire to test a new file-system design, implemented his design on a little used DEC PDP-7. An operating system and command interpreter (shell) was created for this file system. Dennis Ritchie and Rudd Canaday helped create this system named UNICS for "**UN**iplexed **I**nformation and **C**omputing **S**ystem." This name was later changed to UNIX. The PDP-7 version of UNIX was later enchanced to allow two users to work at the same time.

In 1970, Thompson and Dennis Ritchie ported UNIX to a PDP-11/20 to create a text-processing system for internal use. This was a difficult process, and as a result the operating system was rewritten in 1972 to use a high-level language called NB. This was baded on BCPL and is the predecessor of the C programming language developed by Ritchie.

By 1972, UNIX systems were doing word processing at AT&T Bell Laboratories and work scheduling for AT&T in South Carolina. Universities adopted it straight from the laboratory, and external

---

*UNIX is a registered trademark of UNIX System Laboratories, Inc.

licensing began in 1975. By the early 1980s UNIX systems were running throughout the world on thousands of machines ranging from mainframes to microcomputers.

Berkeley has become a major center of UNIX development. Ken Thompson taught an operating system course at the University of California at Berkeley. While at Berkeley, he ported UNIX to a PDP-11/70. The involvement of many students at Berkeley had a major impact on UNIX.

At this time, DARPA (Department of Defense Advanced Research Project Agency) wanted a single operating system to run their AI, VLSI, and Vision work. Eventually, their decision was narrowed down to VMS or UNIX. UNIX was preferred, but the AT&T version of UNIX lacked a major DARPA requirement of virtual memory. At this time, Bill Joy at Berkeley was implementing virtual memory on Berkeley's version of UNIX. DARPA helped support a Berkeley version of UNIX.

With support from many other universities and DARPA, Berkeley released version 3BSD (Berkeley Standard Distribution). This version added the curses terminal package, the vi editor, and virtual memory. Adding virtual memory made Berkeley UNIX a big hit with universities because many users and programs could run at the same time on computers with small memory space.

The Berkeley group, led by Professor William Fabry, added several new features, including the C shell interface. BSD 4.1 software was released in 1981. BSD 4.2 (released in 1983) significantly modified the interprocess communication, networking, and interrupt handling. BSD 4.3 (1986) added some new features and fixed some of the bugs in BSD 4.2. The history of UNIX has had a large impact on its current implementation and use. To this day, most universities use Berkeley UNIX, whereas most corporations use AT&T UNIX. Many universities are connected to the ARPAnet network.

Most UNIX systems are based on Berkeley UNIX or AT&T UNIX. In 1984, AT&T was split up into several companies by the federal government, and the new AT&T was allowed to enter the computer market. In the 1980s, many computer manufacturers adapted AT&T UNIX to run on their systems. Some systems, such as HP-UX (Hewlett-Packard), AIX (IBM), A/UX (Apple), are based on AT&T UNIX and added some Berkeley UNIX features. Some versions of UNIX, ACIS (IBM), and Ultrix (DEC) are based on Berkeley UNIX and have added some AT&T features.

Several other versions of UNIX exist, including Mach and XENIX. The Mach version of UNIX was created by Carnegie-Mellon University and is used on the NeXT computer. It is based on Berkeley UNIX, with modifications to the memory management and interprocess communication. Mach is the successor to Accent, an operating system to study interprocess communication and multiprocessor architecture. The personal computer version of UNIX, called **XENIX**, was developed as a joint project of Microsoft and a corporation called the Santa Cruz Operation. It is very popular on personal computers.

Computer manufacturers are pushing to create a standard version of UNIX. They want to lower costs by not having to support several versions of UNIX, and they want programs compatible among different hardware vendors. Two proposed standards are the POSIX design from the Open Software Foundation (IBM, DEC, HP) and the proposed design from SUN and AT&T. It is uncertain what effect this will have on the future of UNIX.

ABOUT THIS BOOK

This book is designed to take a student with little or no knowledge of UNIX and teach:

1. UNIX commands
2. Shell programming, and
3. UNIX application programming in the C language

This book is based on the lecture notes of the Introduction to UNIX and C class at Stanford University.

## PART ONE

BASIC UNIX COMMANDS

GETTING IN AND OUT OF THE SYSTEM

To use a Unix system, you must log in to the computer, which requires a **login name** and **password**. Your login name consists of 1 to 8 alphanumeric characters; the first character must be alphabetic. You must know your initial password to log in to your account. For security reasons, most system managers are not willing to set up an account without a password—even for a short amount of time.

It is very important to remember that Unix is a case-sensitive system. An uppercase letter is different from a lowercase letter. Both login names and passwords are case sensitive. Login names are usually all lowercase letters. If your login name is myname and you try to login as MYNAME, the system will reject your log-in attempts.

Once connected to the system, you will first be asked for your login name. The prompt looks like:

```
login:
```

Type in your login name and press RETURN. If you mistype your login name before pressing RETURN, you can type a cntl-c and type in your full login name again.

After you have typed in your login name, you will be prompted for your password:

```
password:
```

Type in your password and press RETURN. The password will not appear on the screen when you type it.

If your login was not successful, either the login name or password was not correct. The system will go back and prompt you again for the login and password.

Unix allows you to change what happens when you log in to the system. Chapter 8 on hidden files shows how to do this. What happens right after you log in varies among different computer systems. Most of them will:

- Print a message of the day
- Tell you if electronic mail has been sent to you
- Ask you what type of terminal you are using

Finally, you will receive a prompt. Again, you can redefine what your prompt looks like. Usually, it is a > or a %. Sometimes, the name of the machine you are working on or your login name is printed in front of the >.

CHANGING THE PASSWORD

Once you have a prompt, you can start typing in commands. If you are assigned an initial password, you should change it as soon as possible with the passwd command. Type passwd at the prompt.

```
passwd
```

The passwd command will prompt you for the following information:

```
Old password:
New password:
Retype new password:
```

Enter your current password as the old password.

If you do not remember your current password, passwd will say Sorry and not allow you to change your password. If you do not retype your new password exactly the same way both times, passwd will say Mismatch--password unchanged.

Unix uses a password encryption scheme based on the National Bureau of Standard's Data Encryption Standard. The encrypted form of your password is stored in a file called /etc/passwd that can be read by anyone. The password encryption scheme works best when passwords are 6 to 8 characters in length. If you type in a password that is less than 6 characters in length, passwd will ask you to Please use a longer password .

USING COMMON PASSWORDS

Do not use passwords that are easy to guess. Forget about using your nickname, the type of car you drive, your favorite hobby, your hometown, and anything else related to you. Do not use any word in the English dictionary. A favorite "brute force" approach is to try every word in the online dictionary to see if it is a valid password for some account. Some Unix systems have a program called **insecure** or **secure** that does this. The program can only be used by the system manager, but several people have written their own version of this program!

Try using a special character, preferably in the middle of the password, for additional protection. The password chicago is not safe, but chica.go should be fine. Capital letters in the middle of the password also make it more secure. ChiCago is much more secure than Chicago. Nonobvious numbers in a password also help, as in chicago4.

DEFINING SHELL VARIABLES

When you log in to a system, a program called the **shell** is run to provide you with an interface to the Unix operating system. This shell is responsible for prompting you to type in commands. The shell is discussed in more detail in later chapters.

Shells are briefly mentioned in this chapter, because your terminal type must be set correctly. The setenv command sets a shell environment variable. The TERM variable contains the correct terminal type. To set your terminal type, use:

```
setenv TERM <terminal type>
```

where <terminal type> is the correct terminal type you are using. For example:

```
setenv TERM vt100
```

Case is very important! The setenv must be lowercase, and the TERM must be uppercase. Failure to set the terminal type correctly may cause bizarre output results.

CORRECTING TYPING MISTAKES

While typing in a command, it is possible to make a typing mistake. Assuming the terminal type is set correctly, a cntl-h will delete the last character in a line, cntl-w will delete the last word in a line, and cntl-u will delete the entire line. Either the delete or backspace key will do the same as a cntl-h.

ONLINE HELP

All the documentation about the Unix system is available using the online help facility. Every topic has a man page describing it; Commands have a man page describing how they work, and system calls have a man page describing how to use them.

Each man page is indexed by the name of the command or system call and a one-line description of what it does. Suppose that you want to find out how to check the spelling of a document. Searching through the online manual for the keyword spell will list every man page that has the word spell in the title or one-line description. Each line displayed gives:

- Title
- Section number in parenthesis
- Purpose of the command

To search for a certain keyword, type:

```
man -k keyword
```

To search for all topics related to spell checking, use:

```
man -k spell
```

This spell example produces:

```
spell (1) - find spelling errors
```

To display the actual man page, type:

```
man section topic
```

In this case:

```
man 1 spell
```

If you do not type in a section number, the sections will be searched in order (1,2,3,...) for the topic.

To find out more information about the online help facility, type:

```
man man
```

The information from executing this command is shown in Figure 1.1. Some important things to notice:

1. There are several different sections of the online manual. This man document is located in section 1 of the manual because it says `MAN(1)` at the top of the manual page. There is another manual page titled `''man''` in section 7 of the manual describing how to create manual pages. The man command goes through the sections in order (1,2,3 ...), so man(1) will be chosen instead of man(7) when man man is typed.

2. Anything in `[ ]` brackets is optional. Throughout this book and the online manual, `[ ]` means the argument to the command is optional. For example:

   ```
   man [section] topic
   ```

   This means that the section number is optional. Because man is in section 1 of the manual, you could have typed:

   ```
   man man
   ```        "man title" format

   or

   ```
   man 1 man
   ```        "man section title" format

   You do not need to give the section unless manual pages for that title are located in more than one section.

3. The man command has several options associated with it. In Unix, options are specified with a `-` , followed by a single letter option (`-f, -k, -M`).

4. The man command allows you to look for information about a command without knowing the name of the command. The statement:

   ```
   man -k manual
   ```

   prints a list of all manual pages that have `''manual''` in their name or description:

NAME

>   man - find manual information by keywords; print out the
>   manual

SYNOPSIS

>   man [-] [-M path] [section] title ...
>   man -k keyword ...
>   man -f file ...

DESCRIPTION

Man is a program that gives information from the programmer's manual. It can be asked for one-line descriptions of commands specified by name, or for all commands whose description contains any of a set of keywords. It can also provide online access to the sections of the printed manual.

When given the option -k and a set of keywords, man prints out a one-line synopsis of each manual sections whose listing in the table of contents contains one of those keywords.

When given the option -f and a list of file names, man attempts to locate manual sections related to those files, printing out the table of contents lines for those sections.

When neither -k nor -f is specified, man formats a specified set of manual pages. If a section specifier is given, man looks in that section of the manual for the given titles. Section is either an arabic section number (3 for instance), or one of the words "new", "local", "old", or "public". A section number may be followed by a single-letter classifier (for instance, 1g, indicating a graphics program in section 1). If a section is omitted, man searches all sections of the manual, giving preference to commands over subroutines in system libraries, and printing the first section it finds, if any.

If the standard output is a teletype, or if the flag - is given, man pipes its output through more(1) with the option -s to crush out useless blank lines and to stop after each page on the screen. Hit a space to continue, a control-D to scroll 11 more lines when the output stops.

Normally man checks in a standard location for manual information (/usr/man). This can be changed by supplying a search path (à la the shell) with the -M flag. The search path is a colon-(':') separated list of directories in which manual subdirectories may be found; for example, "/usr/local:/usr/man". If the environment variable 'MAN-PATH' is set, its value is used for the default path. If a search path is supplied with the -k or -f options, it must be specified first.

MAN(1)   UNIX Programmer's Manual   MAN(1)

Man will look for the manual page in either of two forms, the nroff source or pre-formatted pages. If either version is available, the manual page will be displayed. If the preformatted version is available, and it has a more recent modify time than the nroff source, it will be promptly displayed. Otherwise, the manual page will be formatted with nroff and displayed. If the user has permission, the formatted manual page will be deposited in the proper place, so that later invocations of man will not need to format the page again.

FILES

```
/usr/man            standard manual area
/usr/man/man?/*     directories containing source for manuals
/usr/man/cat?/*     directories containing preformatted pages
/usr/man/whatis     keyword database
```

SEE ALSO

```
apropos(1), more(1), whereis(1), catman(8)
```

BUGS

The manual is supposed to be reproducible either on the phototypesetter or on a typewriter. However, on a typewriter some information is necessarily lost.

FIGURE 1.1

catman (8)	Create the cat files for the manual
man (1)	Find manual information by keywords; print out the manual
man (7)	Macros to typeset manual
route (8C)	Manually manipulate the routing tables
whereis (1)	Locate source, binary, and or manual for program

5. When you have more than one screenful of information, paging is done through the more command. Under the control of more, the screen will stop until the space bar is typed.

LOGGING OUT OF THE COMPUTER

To log out of the computer, type logout. If you get a message saying there are stopped jobs, type logout a second time.

EXERCISES

1. Using the online manual, how do you find out which editors are available? *Strong hint*: Search for the keyword editor.   □

2. Using the online manual, how do you find out what command is used to list files?   □

3. Which of the following passwords are valid:

   3.1   Chi.cago
   3.2   Detroit
   3.3   unix
   3.4   1porsche
   3.5   chicago
   3.6   benzene   □

4. Assuming all the above passwords are valid, which ones can be considered secure? Explain your reasoning.   □

FILE AND DIRECTORY COMMANDS

In the early 1970s, Ken Thompson wanted to test a file-system design; Unix was built around this experiment. The result is an excellent file-system design, which has been a model for many other operating systems.

Some primary advantages of the Unix file system are:

- Easy to use directories
- Simple and effective file-protection scheme
- Uses byte-stream model
- Hardware devices directly accessible through the file system.

One of the major advantages of Unix is its hierarchic file system. It is a tree of directories and files. The directory at the top of the tree is called the **root directory**, which is denoted by a single / . Inside each of these directories can be subdirectories and files. In Unix, some of the subdirectories under the root directory are **/etc**, **/usr**, and **/dev**. Under /usr exist subdirectories such as **/bin**, **/ucb**, and **/local**. Under /bin are some executable files such as **who**. (The who command prints out who is working on the system.)

Here is an example of the tree in Unix starting from the root directory:

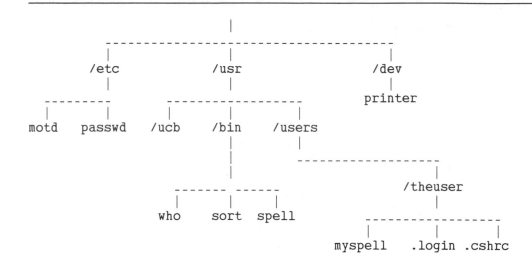

In Unix, to run a command, you can specify the pathname and then the name of the command. The pathname tells the computer how to look down the directory tree. In this example, the pathname is /usr/bin and the name of the command is who. Specifying /usr/bin/who runs the who program. Just typing the name of the command searches through a predefined set of directories to find the correct program to execute. To change the set of predefined directories, refer to Chapter 8 on hidden files.

FILE COMMANDS

Home Directory

When your Unix account is created, a home directory is set up for you. Every time you log in to the system, you start in your home directory. The location of your home directory varies among different computers, but in this example, it is located in /usr/users. The names of the subdirectories in /usr/users are the same as the login names. In this example, the home directory for the user with the login name theuser is /usr/users/theuser.

All home directories have two files, .login and .cshrc, which describe what happens when you log in to the system. In addition to these two files, this user has a file called **myspell** in the home directory.

Absolute Pathnames

In Unix, all the pathnames can be absolute or relative. Absolute means to start from the root directory. Absolute pathnames start with a beginning / such as /usr/bin/who. With absolute filenames, the entire directory path is specified starting with the root directory.

Relative Pathnames

Relative pathnames start from the directory in which you are currently located. These pathnames do not begin with a / . For example, if you are in the /usr directory, the relative path name to run the who command is bin/who .

Specifiying ../ within a filename goes up one directory. From the /usr/ucb directory, the relative pathname ../bin/who executes the who command. The ../ goes up to the /usr directory, and the bin/who executes the who command.

The symbol ~ always refers to your home directory. No matter where you are in the filesystem, ~/myspell is the file in your home directory. To reference a file in some other user's directory, use:

```
~username/filename
```

ls: Listing Files

The ls command lists the files in your directory. The format of this command is:

```
ls [options] filenames(s)
```

For each filename listed, if it is a file, information about that file is displayed. If the filename is a directory, information about all the files and subdirectories in that directory are displayed.

If no options are specified, ls will only display the names of the files and subdirectories. To display additional information, some options must be specified. The ls command has many options associated with it. Some of the most useful are:

- -l : Prints detail information about each file. It shows the following information:
  1. File protection for each file (read, write, and execute permission for the owner of the file, people in the same group, and then anyone else)
  2. Number of files in the subdirectory (if it is a subdirectory)

3. Owner of the file
4. Size of file in bytes
5. Date the file was last modified
6. Name of the file

For example, ls -l /usr/users/theuser shows:

```
-rw-------   1 theuser       516 May 20 13:54 myspell
```

The user named theuser can read and write this file; no one else can read or write it (file permission is explained later in this chapter). It shows the number 1 because myspell is a file and is not a subdirectory with some number of files underneath it. This user (theuser) owns the file. It is 516 bytes long and was created on May 20th.

- -t : Lists the files in order by modification date
- -g : Shows what group owns the file (see chmod for more information)
- -a : Shows hidden files in addition to regular files.

All filenames that begin with a . are called **hidden files**. These are files that you normally do not want to be listed, such as .login and .cshrc. Hidden files are described in Chapter 8.

The command ls -a /usr/users/theuser shows:

```
.cshrc   .login   myspell
```

Options can be combined, and it makes no difference in what order you specify the options. ls -latg /usr/users/theuser shows:

```
-rw-rw-r--  1 theuser    student 516 May 20 13:54 myspell
-rwx------  1 theuser    student 807 May 12 12:02 .cshrc
-rwx------  1 theuser    student 495 Apr 22 09:31 .login
```

cat and more : Show File Contents

Both the **cat** and the **more** command can be used to show the contents of a file on your terminal screen. To show the contents of the /etc/motd file, you can do either:

```
cat /etc/motd
```

or

```
more /etc/motd
```

On files smaller than the size of your screen, cat and more work the same way; they differ on how they display files longer than the length of your terminal, such as the file /etc/rc.

A cat /etc/rc will display the entire contents of the file on your screen at once. To stop this listing, type a cntl-s. A cntl-w continues displaying the file. The cat command is not a very useful way to show your file. It is useful in conjunction with other commands.

The more command is a better way to show your file if it is larger than the size of your screen. Typing more /etc/rc shows the first 24 lines of the file (assuming your terminal has 24 lines) and then displays:

```
--More--(0%)
```

The number before the percent symbol tells what percent of the file has been seen.

At this point, if you press RETURN, you will scroll up one line of the file. Press the space bar to scroll up one screen. Type q to quit. A number followed by the RETURN key will display that number of lines. Typing h displays a summary of all the possible options.

cp : Copy Files

The cp command copies files. The format of the cp command is:

```
cp [options] from-file to-file
```

or

```
cp [options] from-file(s) to-directory
```

The first form of the cp command copies from from-file to to-file in the same directory. The second form of the command shows how to copy one or more files into another directory. The cp command has several options:

- -r : Recursive. Will recursively copy the files in all the subdirectories.
- -i : Interactive. If copying the file, it will overwrite an old version of a file. The -i option asks if you want to do the copy. Without the option, it will just overwrite the file without asking.
- -p : Preserve the permission modes and modification times of the files

mv : Move Files

To move a file instead of copying it, use the mv command. The mv command can do two things:

1. It can move a file or directory to another directory
2. It can rename a file or directory

The format for moving a file or directory is:

```
mv [options] filename todirectoryname
```

or

```
mv [options] directoryname todirectoryname
```

The format for renaming a file or directory is:

```
mv [options] oldfilename newfilename
```

or

```
mv [options] olddirectoryname newdirectoryname
```

The directory todirectoryname must exist to actually move the file or directory. If it does not, the mv command assumes that you are renaming the file or directory.

The mv command has two important options:

- -i : Interactive. If moving the file will overwrite another file, the -i option will cause you to be asked if you want to do the move. Without the option, it will just overwrite the file without asking.
- -f : Force. Overrides any file permission mode restrictions if you are the owner of the file being overwritten.

rm : Remove Files

Unix handles file removal with the rm command by physically deleting your file. Once you remove a file with rm, you can never get it back except to restore it from a dump tape. Seriously consider creating a directory called trash in your home directory and moving files to this directory instead of deleting the files with rm. The format of rm is:

```
rm [options] filename(s)
```

Be careful when using the -r and -f options:

- -r : Recursive. Recursively removes all the files and subdirectories
- -i : Interactive. Will ask for each file whether or not you want to remove it
- -f : Force. Will override any file permission mode restrictions if you are the owner of the file being deleted

FILE PROTECTION

You can specify the permission of a file or directory:

1. r : Read permission
2. w : Write permission
3. x : Execute permission

Permission	File	Directory
r	Read the file	List files in directory
w	Rewrite or remove file	Remove any file in directory Put a file in the directory Remove the directory itself
x	Run executable program	Read, write, or execute any files in the directory

These permissions can be specified for each of the following categories:

1. u : The user—the owner of the file
2. g : All members in the same group as the owner of the file
3. o : All other people

The ls -l command shows these permissions in order by user, group, and others:

```
-rw-rw-r--  1 theuser        516 May 20 13:54 myspell
-rwx------  1 theuser        807 May 12 12:02 .cshrc
-rwx------  1 theuser        495 Apr 22 09:31 .login
```

This user has read, write, and execute permissions for the .login and .cshrc files. Anyone in his group can read and write the myspell file, and anyone on the system can read it.

CHMOD : CHANGE FILE PERMISSION MODES

The chmod command is used to change your file or directory permission mode. The format of the chmod command is:

```
chmod mode filename
```

The mode consists of:

Category + permission to add permission, or
Category − permission to delete permission

For example:

chmod o+w myspell   Allow anyone to write the file myspell. Write permission allows the file to be changed or removed.

chmod u-r myspell   Not allow the owner to read the myspell file.

If your directory permission forbids write access, a file may not be written or deleted in the directory—no matter what the permission of the file. A directory must have access permission to read, write, or execute a file in the directory.

NUMERIC PERMISSION MODES

Another form of the chmod command allows an octal number to be used for the mode. This number has the values:

Value	Meaning
4	Read permission allowed
2	Write permission allowed
1	Execute permission allowed

A value of six (4 + 2) allows read and write permission. A value of five (4 + 1) allows read and execute permission. The numeric form for the mode of the chmod command has three digits for:

1. Permission for the owner of the file or directory
2. Group permission of the file or directory
3. Permission for anyone on the system

For example, the command:

chmod 700 /usr/users/theuser

allows this user to do anything in the home directory while no one else may use the directory in any manner. The command:

chmod 644 ~/thedata

allows the owner to read or write the file, everyone else may only read the file.

UMASK : DEFAULT FILE PERMISSION

The umask command gives the default file protection mode when a new file or directory is created. The numeric value to give umask is:

```
??? - permissionvalue
```

where permissionvalue is the numeric mode of the chmod command. Read only permission is $7 - 4 = 3$. Read and write permission is $7 - (4 + 2) = 1$.

The values of umask are the permissions for the user, group, and others. For example, a mode of 755 gives the user read, write, and execute permission, whereas group and others have read and execute permission. Therefore, the command:

```
umask 022
```

sets the default mode of all files and directories created to read, write, and execute permission for the user, whereas group and others have read and execute permission. This default permission (755) is given because $777 - 755 = 022$.

DIRECTORY COMMANDS

Subdirectories

Instead of putting all your files in your home directory, Unix allows you to create subdirectories and put files in them. Subdirectories allow your files to be organized much better than putting all of them in your home directory. Logically related files should be stored in the same subdirectory. For example, you might have a subdirectory called letters to keep all your letters. Your memos directory might contain all your memos.

cd Change Directory

The cd command changes the current directory where you are located. The format of the cd command is:

```
cd directoryname
```

If no directoryname is specified, your current directory becomes your home directory. The directoryname can be an absolute or relative pathname. A few sample uses of the cd command:

```
cd              Go to your home directory
cd /usr/bin     Go to the /usr/bin directory
cd ~/letters    Go to your letters subdirectory
```

mkdir Make Directories

The mkdir command is used to make a directory. The format of mkdir is:

```
mkdir directoryname
```

To make a letters subdirectory from your home directory, type:

```
mkdir letters
```

Nested Subdirectories

To create two subdirectories called personal and business in your letters directory, use:

```
mkdir ~/letters/personal
mkdir ~/letters/business
```

pwd Print Working Directory

The pwd command prints out the full pathname of the directory in which you are located. This command is very useful if you forget what directory you are located in.

EXERCISES

Use the following file system for the exercise questions:

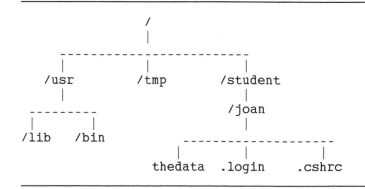

1. Specify three ways that Joan may go from the /usr/bin directory to her home directory (/student/joan), using the cd command. ☐

2. Using the cp command, how can Joan copy the file thedata into the /tmp directory? This should work no matter where she is located in the directory tree. ☐

3. Instead of using the rm command to remove the file thedata, how can she move the file to the /tmp directory? Again, this should work no matter where she is in the directory tree. ☐

4. Joan decides she does not want to use the rm command. Instead, she will create a subdirectory in her home directory called trash and move all the files she wants to delete to this trash directory. Assuming she starts in her home directory, show how she can create a trash directory and move the file thedata to the trash subdirectory. ☐

5. How can Joan change the protection on the file thedata so that anyone in her group can read the file? ☐

6. How can Joan modify the permission on her home directory, so that:

   • She can read, write, and execute files in the directory, and
   • No one else may read, write, or execute any files in her directory? ☐

7. If Joan sets the protection of her home directory so that no one except herself may read, write, or execute files in it, will adding permission for anyone to read the file thedata allow anyone (except Joan) to read it? ☐

8. Where is your home directory located? Give the full pathname. What files are located in your directory, including hidden files? ☐

9. How would you set up your default permission mode so that you and anyone in your group has read and execute permission while all others would only have read permission? How would you test it to make certain it works correctly? ☐

EDITING FILES

On Unix systems, there are three main families of editors: ed, vi, and emacs. The ed editor was the first of these three editors created. It is a line oriented editor instead of a full-screen editor and is very primitive compared to vi and emacs. The ed editor is rarely used anymore. The most useful application of ed is when you need to edit a file and you are not on a full-screen editor device, such as a console terminal.

To find out more about the ed editor, look at the online manual (man ed), which has a very detailed description.

Vi and emacs are much more popular than the ed editor. Both are full-screen editors, but vi is historically based on the ed editor. Take ed, add full-screen editing and some other features, and you have vi. Ed commands can be used inside of the vi editor.

There are a variety of emacs editors. Emacs editors rely on control key and escape key sequences to manipulate text. My favorite version of emacs is gnuemacs. It is very powerful, works on many different architectures, and is public domain software.

The major difference among the many versions of emacs is the key sequences to perform some functions. Most of the key sequences described here for gnuemacs work for other versions of emacs.

VI

The vi editor has two major advantages over emacs:

1. Emacs requires more cpu and memory space to edit a file.
2. The vi editor is available on every Unix system.

The format of the vi command is:

```
vi filename
```

The vi editor has two modes. They are **insert mode**, where the characters you type are inserted into the file, and **command mode**, where the characters you type are commands for the vi editor to execute. Vi initially starts up in command mode. To get into insert mode from command mode, type i. The ESC key goes from insert mode to command mode.

Some lines on the screen may contain the ~ character. These are lines that are past the end of your buffer—they do not show up in the file. The last line on your screen is a status line to display messages and enter certain commands.

Movement Commands

The following commands allow movement when editing your file.

Screen Movement

- cntl-U : Scroll up
- cntl-D : Scroll down
- cntl-F : Scroll forward
- cntl-B : Scroll backward

Line Movement

- j : Move down one line
- k : Move up one line
- H : Move to first line on screen
- M : Move to the middle line on the screen
- L : Move to last line on the screen
- h : Move left one character
- l or space : Move right one character
- ^ : Move to the beginning of a line
- $: Move to the end of a line
- kG : Go to line k
- G : Go to the end of the file
- . : Repeat last edit (change, deletion) command

Deletion and Insertion Commands

Deletion Commands

- ndd : Delete next n lines
- nx : Delete next n characters

- `nX` : Delete previous n characters
- `D` : Delete from current position to end of line

Typing a `d` followed by any movement command deletes text in the area from the current position to the new position. For example, `dG` deletes to the end of the file. A `d$` deletes to the end of line.

The last text that you deleted is stored in a deleted text buffer. This deleted text can be inserted back into the document by using the `p` command.

To move text, delete the text that you want moved, move your cursor where you want it placed, and type `p` to insert the text. To duplicate text, delete the text, type `p` to yank it back, move your cursor where you want the duplicate to appear, and type `p` a second time.

Saving and Inserting Files

The following commands are associated with saving edited information to a file. All of them except ZZ must be ended by typing the return key.

- `:w` : Write buffer back to file
- `:w file` : Write buffer to file
- `:w! file` : Write buffer to file even if it already exists
- `:q` : Quit
- `:q!` : Quit—discarding changes
- `ZZ` : Save buffer and exit
- `:r file` : To insert a file in the buffer
- `:vi file` : To edit a new file

Searching

These commands search for a certain string. The return key must be pressed after both these commands:

- `/string` : Forward search
- `?string` : Backward search

To continue searching:

- `n` : Searches for the next occurrence of the string
- `N` : Reverses direction and searches for the next occurrence

Using ed Commands

All the ed editing commands may be used in vi. Typing ":" allows vi to use any ed editing command. To substitute text in vi (and ed), use:

```
:first,last s/text/substitution/g
```

where:

- `first` is the first line number
- `last` is the last line number
- `text` is the text you want substituted
- `substitution` is the text you want substituted

EMACS

Emacs is a full-screen editor to modify buffers of text. The contents of a file are read into the buffer, and the buffer contents are written back to a file.

To run emacs, specify:

```
emacs
```

or you can optionally specify a filename after emacs. This file is loaded into the buffer when emacs is started up.

Emacs Filename

The examples shown in this section use gnuemacs. Other versions of emacs work in a similar manner. On some systems, emacs will run a different version of emacs. To run the gnuemacs version, you may have to type gnuemacs instead of emacs.

Emacs Windows

Running emacs creates a window on your screen containing:

- Text window showing the contents of the buffer
- A one-line mode line describing what is going on in the text window
- A minibuffer—a special location to input commands

This window is shown in Figure 3.1.

The mode line describes what is going on in a window. It tells you the name of the buffer (in this case *scratch*), the name of the file that this buffer is associated with (right now there is none), and the mode of the file. An example of a certain mode is the C programming style mode. If you edit a file ending with a .c suffix, emacs executes

```
.-------------------------------------------------------.
|                                                       |
|                                                       |
|                                                       |
|                                                       |
|                                                       |
|                                                       |
|                         .                             |
|                                                       |
|                                                       |
|                                                       |
|                                                       |
|                                                       |
|                                                       |
| ------------------------------------------------------|
|-----Emacs: *scratch*                  ----All---------|
| ------------------------------------------------------|
```

FIGURE 3.1

in C mode. This mode does some things automatically for you, such as indenting brackets.

The mode line also tells how far down in the buffer you are looking. All means that the entire buffer fits on one screen. Top means that you are looking at the beginning of the buffer. Bot means that you are looking at the end of the buffer. A number followed by a "%" sign tells you how far the top line of your screen is from the bottom of the buffer.

Escape and Control Keys

Emacs relies heavily on the escape key and the control key. Throughout this chapter, <esc> means to type the escape key and cntl means to press on the control key when typing the letter. For example,

```
<esc> a
```

means to type the escape key and then the a key. This is referred to as an **escape sequence**.

```
cntl-a
```

means to press down on the control key and press a while continuing to hold down the control key. This is known as a **control character**.

If you are not typing an escape sequence or a control character, then the information that you type on your keyboard is inserted into the buffer.

Character Operations

The character operations are:

- `cntl-b` : Move back one character
- `cntl-f` : Mover forward on character
- `cntl-p` : Move to the previous line
- `cntl-n` : Move to the next line
- `cntl-d` : Delete the character underneath the cursor
- `delete` : Delete the character to the left of the cursor
- `cntl-t` : Transpose the two previous characters

File Operations

The file operations are:

- `cntl-x cntl-v` : Visit a file—putting the contents of a file into the buffer
- `cntl-x cntl-w` : Write the contents of the buffer to a file
- `cntl-x cntl-s` : Write the contents of the buffer to the file listed in the mode line

To exit emacs, use the following control sequence:

```
cntl-x cntl-c
```

Line Operations

Line operations work with an entire line of the buffer. The four line operations are:

- `cntl-a` : Move the cursor to the beginning of the line
- `cntl-e` : Move the cursor to the end of the line
- `cntl-o` : Insert a blank line into the buffer
- `cntl-k` : Kill a line of text

Word Operations

Word operations work with an entire word of text at one time instead of just one character at a time.

- `<esc>b` : Move back one word
- `<esc>f` : Move forward one word
- `<esc><delete>` : Delete one word to the left
- `<esc>d` : Delete one word to the right

- <esc>t : Transpose the two words around the cursor
- <esc>c : Capitalize a word. You have to be at the beginning of the word to do this properly.
- <esc>u : Convert a word to uppercase
- <esc>l : Convert a word to lowercase

Sentence Operations

There are also two sentence operations that are similar to the line operations. Emacs interprets the ".", "?", and the "!" characters as sentence delimiters.

- <esc>a : Move to the beginning of a sentence
- <esc>e : Move to the end of a sentence

Screen Manipulation

When your emacs buffer contains more than one screenful of information, it is useful to move through an entire screenful of text at a time.

- cntl-v : View the next screenful of information in the buffer
- <esc>v : View the previous screenful of information in the buffer
- <esc>< : Go to the top of the buffer
- <esc>> : Go to the bottom of the buffer
- cntl-l : Redisplay the screen. This is very useful in cases where something unrelated to your editing appears on the screen, such as a notification that new mail has arrived.

Regions

Emacs allows you to create a region around any part of the text in your buffer. The two most common uses of regions is to delete a large block of text and duplicate a large block of text.

In emacs, the "mark" marks the beginning of a region. Your cursor is the end of a region. To create a region, first move your cursor to the beginning of a region and type:

```
cntl-@
```

This sets the mark at the point where your cursor is located. Move the cursor to the location where you want the region to end.

To delete all the text in the region, type

```
cntl-w
```

This deletes all the text in a region. All the deleted text is put into a special buffer called the **killbuffer**. The previous contents of the killbuffer are removed when new text is put in the killbuffer.

You can copy the contents of the killbuffer back into your buffer with

```
cntl-y
```

The text is inserted back into your buffer at the position where your cursor is located.

To make a copy of a certain part of your text, first delete that part of the text using cntl-@ and cntl-w, and then bring it back (called **yanking**) with cntl-y in the original location. This text is still stored in the killbuffer, so move the cursor to the location where you want the copy to exist and use cntl-y to yank it back again.

Searching in Emacs

When editing text, it is useful to search for a string of characters in the buffer. Emacs allows you to search from the cursor to the beginning of the buffer or from the cursor to the end of the buffer. The control characters to do this are:

- `cntl-s` : Search to the end of the buffer
- `cntl-r` : Search to the beginning of the buffer

As soon as you start your search, the word `I-search` appears in the minibuffer. I-search stands for interactive search. Every time an additional character is typed, emacs continues its search. Whatever is typed in the minibuffer is searched for in the buffer.

When doing an I-search, to find the next occurrence of the string, just type `cntl-s` again. To find the previous occurrence of a string, type `cntl-r` again. Once you have started a search, you can search forward and backward through the buffer with cntl-s and cntl-r.

To get out of search mode, type the <esc> key. This puts you back in editing mode. Typing a control character while in search mode immediately takes you out of search mode—putting you in editing mode and executing the control character that is typed. When you get out of search mode, it sets the mark at that point.

Using Multiple Buffers

Emacs allows multiple buffers to be edited at the same time. However, only one buffer can be selected and visible in a window at one time.

To create and use a new buffer, type

```
cntl-x b
```

The program prompts you to type in the name of the buffer followed by the RETURN key. This buffer is now displayed in your window.

Select a buffer in the same way as creating a buffer. When you type cntl-x b, if a buffer already exists with the name you type in, that buffer is selected. Otherwise, a new buffer is created with that name.

To see a list of all the buffers used, type

```
cntl-x cntl-b
```

Two windows are displayed after doing this. The text being edited is shown in the top window. The bottom window shows the following information for each buffer:

- ** Shows up if the buffer has been modified since it was last saved
- Buffer name
- Size of the buffer
- The mode of the buffer (such as C mode)
- The file associated with a buffer

To go back to editing your file in a single window, type:

```
cntl-x 1
```

(See the next section on multiple windows for more information.)
To kill a buffer, type:

```
cntl-x k
```

This asks you which buffer you would like to kill. All the text in this buffer is stored in the killbuffer.

To copy text between buffers, you must delete a region of text in one buffer to store the text in the killbuffer and insert it in the other buffer with a cntl-y.

Multiple Windows

Emacs can split the screen into two windows. These two windows can display two different parts of the same buffer or display two different buffers.

- `cntl-x 2` : Start showing two windows
- `cntl-x 1` : Start showing just one window again. The window to show is the one where the cursor is located
- `cntl-x 0` : Delete this window
- `cntl-x o` : Switch the cursor to the other window
- `cntl-u cntl-x 2` : Show two windows with the same buffer in both windows

One of the most common uses of multiple windows is to look at a file of errors (such as compile errors) in one window while editing a document (such as the program) in the other window.

Specifying Numeric Arguments

Any emacs control character or escape sequence can be given a repetition factor. To repeat a control character or escape sequence a certain number of times, type `cntl-u`, followed by the number of times you want to perform an operation, followed by the control character or escape sequence. For example, typing

```
cntl-u 10 cntl-p
```

moves you back 10 lines because cntl-p moves you back one line.

The most common use of numeric arguments is to go to a certain line number. To get to a certain line number in emacs, first type <esc>c to get to the top of the buffer. Then, type:

```
cntl-u
```

the line number you want to go to

```
cntl-n
```

SUMMARY

Both vi and emacs are full-screen editors allowing a user to edit files. The vi editor is available on all Berkeley Unix systems, whereas emacs is not available on all systems. The choice of which editor to use depends on the user.

CHAPTER 4

C SHELL INTERFACE

The C shell (csh) is your interface to the Unix system and is responsible for interpreting your keyboard input. When you log in to a Unix system, the shell is started and runs until you log out of the system. The shell is a very powerful program allowing:

1. Connection of the output of one command as input to a second command
2. The output of commands to be sent to files
3. Files as input to commands
4. Multiple commands running at the same time
5. Aliasing the names of commands
6. Ease of running commands you have previously executed

PIPES AND FILE REDIRECTION

Standard Input, Output, and Error

Every command has three "files" associated with it called **standard input**, **standard output**, and **standard error**. Input may be read from standard input, output may be sent to standard output, and error messages are sent to standard error. By default, your standard input file is the terminal keyboard, and standard output and standard error are the terminal screen. These default devices may be changed using one of the following special shell symbols:

| | & < > >> >&

File Redirection

The C shell interprets the following symbols as file redirection symbols:

<   Use file as standard input
>   Use file as standard output
>>   Append standard output to the file
>&   Write both standard error and standard output to the file.

For example, to compile a program and send the compiler errors to a file called cmperrs:

```
cc filename.c >& cmperrs
```

To sort the contents of myfile and put the output into a file called sortedfile:

```
sort < myfile > sortedfile
```

Pipes

A pipe takes the standard output of one process and makes it the standard input of another process. Use a pipe in the following manner to send the standard output of command1 as the standard input of command2.

```
command1 | command2
```

For example, to produce a sorted list of who is on the system, type:

```
who | sort
```

A pipe is very useful if the standard output of any command produces more lines of output than the size of your terminal. The output can be piped to the more command to stop it from scrolling off the screen. For example:

```
who | more
```

More than one pipe at the same time is allowed. To display a sorted list of users on the system running emacs:

```
who | grep emacs | sort | more
```

Very few commands send output to standard error. One of these is the C programming language compiler, which sends compiler error messages to standard error. To stop these messages after every screenful of information, you must use the | & symbol:

```
cc filename.c |& more
```

RUNNING MULTIPLE JOBS

The C shell allows several commands to be running at the same time. A command is running in either the foreground mode or the background mode. When the shell is running a command in the foreground mode, the shell waits for the command to finish before prompting the user for the next command. If a command is running in the background mode, the shell does not wait for the command to finish before prompting the user for the next command to enter. Therefore, only one job can be running in the foreground while multiple jobs can run in the background. Background jobs can run while a foreground job is executing.

Just typing the name of the command runs it in the foreground. Typing a & after the name of a command runs it in the background.

A job is in one of three states: foreground mode, background mode, or stopped mode. **Foreground mode** means that it is executing in the foreground, and **background mode** means that it is executing in the background. **Stopped mode** means that a job previously executing in foreground mode has been stopped by the user. Stopped jobs will remain stopped until the user brings them into foreground or background mode.

The jobs command lists all the commands you have running in the background. It tells:

- background-job-number: This is different from the process id
- Whether it is running or stopped
- Name of the command

To bring a background job to the foreground, type:

```
fg %background-job-number
```

To make the foreground command stopped in the background, type a cntl-z while the command is running.

To make a stopped job start running in the background, type:

```
bg %background-job-number
```

Figure 4.1 shows an example of running multiple commands at the same time.

```
> sleep 30000 &

[1] 5946

> cat > foo.c

cntl-Z
Stopped
> jobs

[1] - Running              sleep 30000
[2] + Stopped              cat > foo.c

> sort /etc/passwd | more &

[3] 5948 5949

> jobs
```

Note: The sort command is stopped because it is waiting for the user to press the space bar
to display the next page of information.

```
[1]   Running              sleep 30000
[2] - Stopped              cat > foo.c
[3] + Stopped (tty output) sort /etc/passwd : more

> fg %2
cat > foo.c

cntl-D

> jobs

[1] - Running              sleep 30000
[3] + Stopped (tty output) sort /etc/passwd | more

> fg
sort /etc/passwd | more

jw:**password here**:107:31:James Wilson:/user/jw:/bin/csh
root:**password here**:0:10:root account:/:/bin/csh

> fg %1
sleep 30000
<cntl-c>
```

Note: <cntl-c> means to press the control and the c keys at the same time.

FIGURE 4.1

Running a job in the background shows the job number in brackets and the process-id number of the job. The jobs command shows a "+" by the most recently executed job and a "-" by the second most recently executed job. The jobs command also shows if any background job is stopped because it needs to display output on the terminal. Running the fg command without specifying a job number runs the most recently stopped job.

ALIASING COMMAND NAMES

The alias command redefines the names of Unix commands. The format of the alias command is:

```
alias newname command-statement
```

For example, on DEC TOPS-20 computers, the command dir lists the names of your files and the vdir command lists the names of your files and information about them. Anyone coming from a TOPS-20 environment may prefer the names dir and vdir. To use these names, just type:

```
alias dir "ls"
alias vdir "ls -l"
```

From this point, every time dir is typed, the ls command is executed. The command statement allows any of the special shell symbols:

```
alias w "/usr/ucb/w | more"
alias lsandpwd "(ls ; pwd) &"
```

After creating these aliases, typing w runs the program

```
/usr/ucb/w
```

and pipes the output to the more command. With this alias, the full pathname of the command must be given because the same name as the program is used for the alias. The alias lsandpwd executes a job in the background. This job runs the ls command and then the pwd command.

C SHELL VARIABLES

Several variables are associated exclusively with the C shell. Use the set command to assign values to these variables. The format of the set command is:

```
set variable = value
```

To set your prompt to Howdy, use:

```
set prompt = "Howdy"
```

Instead of setting your prompt to some fixed string (Howdy), the prompt variable may be set to the output of some Unix command. The statement:

```
set prompt = "'command'"
```

executes the command, and the backquotes around it puts the output of the command in the string. For example, users on a workstation sometimes connect to three or four systems at the same time. It is important for their prompt to tell which system they are working on. The hostname command tells what system a user is working on.

The following command sets the C shell prompt to the name of the machine:

```
set prompt = "'hostname'"
```

HISTORY

Another important variable to set is the history variable. The C shell remembers the previous commands you have executed. The history variable gives the number of previous commands to remember. This statement causes the shell to remember the past 20 commands:

```
set history=20
```

The command history prints out the previous commands you have executed. Figure 4.2 shows a sample output of executing the history command. In this example, history is the fifth command executed since the user logged in to the system. It shows all the commands executed so far:

```
1  cd scratch
2  ls -lF
3  cat foobar
4  emacs foobar
5  history
```

FIGURE 4.2

REEXECUTING COMMANDS

The "!" character (called the **bang** character) refers to some previously executed command. Typing !! means to execute the previous command again.

Typing

    !string

executes the last command starting with that string.

    !number

executes that command number again. In the previous example, typing !c or !3 executes the command cat foobar. Typing !cd executes the command cd scratch.

SUMMARY

The shell interface is the interface to the Unix system. It allows file redirection for input and output to commands, output of one command as input to another command, multiple commands to be running at the same time, command names aliased to another name, and remembering a history of commands previously executed.

EXERCISES

1. Give a one-line command sequence to produce a sorted list of users on the system and write this output to a file called sortedlist. Use the sort command to sort the output produced by the who command.   □

2. If a user logs into a Unix system and types the following input to the shell, list the commands executed by the shell for each of the history substitutions: □

        1>   w
        2>   who
        3>   ls
        4>   !1
        5>   cd /tmp
        6>   !3
        7>   !c
        8>   !w

MISCELLANEOUS UNIX COMMANDS

A variety of commands are covered in the next three chapters. Chapter 6 covers filters. Filters are commands that take some input, transform the data in some manner, and send the transformed data to the output. Chapter 7 covers the file-archiving and networking commands. This chapter covers many of the miscellaneous commands that do not fall into the other categories. The commands discussed in this chapter are:

1. echo: Print a line of output
2. who: Show who is working on the system
3. date: Display the current date
4. cal: Display the calendar
5. bc: Calculator
6. wc: Display number of lines, words, and characters in a file
7. spell: Check the spelling of a document
8. script: Record terminal output in a file
9. printer commands
   9.1 lpr: Print a file
   9.2 lprm: Delete a print request from the print queue
   9.3 lpq: Show printer status

10. Miscellaneous games
11. `uptime`: Show system load and system status
12. `du`: disk usage
13. `nice`: Lower command priority
14. `find`: Find a file in the file system

ECHO: PRINT A LINE

The format of the echo command is:

```
echo [ -n ] [ arg ] . . .
```

Echo writes its arguments separated by blanks and terminated by a newline on the standard output. If the flag −n is used, no newline is added to the output. It is very useful for displaying output in a shell program.

Example Usage

```
> echo this is a line of text
this is a line of text

> echo -n another line
another line>
```

WHO: WHO IS ON THE SYSTEM

The format of the who command is:

```
who
```

This command lists the login name, terminal name, and login time for each user on the system.

Example Usage

```
> who

me      console May 2 21:08
jw      ttya    May 2 14:05
```

DATE: **DISPLAY OR SET CURRENT DATE**

The format of the date command is:

```
date [ -u ] [ yymmddhhmm [ .ss ] ]
```

The command date without any options displays the current date and time. Providing a date value in the form yymmddhhmm or yymmddhhmmss sets the date where:

- yy represents the last two digits of the year
- The first mm is the month number
- dd is the day
- hh is the hour (24-hour system)
- The second mm is the minute
- ss is optional and represents the seconds

Only the root user may set the date.

Date takes care of the conversion to and from local standard and daylight-saving time.

Options

-u Displays or sets the date in GMT (universal) time.

Example Usage

```
> date
Tue May  2 22:20:31 PDT 1989

> date 8506131627
Thur June 13 16:27:00 PDT 1985
```

CAL: **ONLINE CALENDAR**

The format of the cal command is:

```
cal [ month ] year
```

It prints a calendar for the specified year. If a month is also specified, a calendar just for that month is printed. The year can be between 1 and 9999. The full year must be specified—a year value of 89 is the year 89 AD, not 1989 AD.

Example Usage

> cal 1990

1990

```
            JANUARY                      FEBRUARY                      MARCH
      S  M  T  W  T  F  S          S  M  T  W  T  F  S          S  M  T  W  T  F  S
         1  2  3  4  5  6                      1  2  3                         1  2  3
      7  8  9 10 11 12 13          4  5  6  7  8  9 10          4  5  6  7  8  9 10
     14 15 16 17 18 19 20         11 12 13 14 15 16 17         11 12 13 14 15 16 17
     21 22 23 24 25 26 27         18 19 20 21 22 23 24         18 19 20 21 22 23 24
     28 29 30 31                  25 26 27 28                  25 26 27 28 29 30 31

             APRIL                         MAY                          JUNE
      S  M  T  W  T  F  S          S  M  T  W  T  F  S          S  M  T  W  T  F  S
      1  2  3  4  5  6  7                1  2  3  4  5                            1  2
      8  9 10 11 12 13 14          6  7  8  9 10 11 12          3  4  5  6  7  8  9
     15 16 17 18 19 20 21         13 14 15 16 17 18 19         10 11 12 13 14 15 16
     22 23 24 25 26 27 28         20 21 22 23 24 25 26         17 18 19 20 21 22 23
     29 30                        27 28 29 30 31               24 25 26 27 28 29 30

             JULY                        AUGUST                      SEPTEMBER
      S  M  T  W  T  F  S          S  M  T  W  T  F  S          S  M  T  W  T  F  S
      1  2  3  4  5  6  7                   1  2  3  4                            1
      8  9 10 11 12 13 14          5  6  7  8  9 10 11          2  3  4  5  6  7  8
     15 16 17 18 19 20 21         12 13 14 15 16 17 18          9 10 11 12 13 14 15
     22 23 24 25 26 27 28         19 20 21 22 23 24 25         16 17 18 19 20 21 22
     29 30 31                     26 27 28 29 30 31            23 24 25 26 27 28 29
                                                               30

            OCTOBER                      NOVEMBER                     DECEMBER
      S  M  T  W  T  F  S          S  M  T  W  T  F  S          S  M  T  W  T  F  S
         1  2  3  4  5  6                      1  2  3                            1
      7  8  9 10 11 12 13          4  5  6  7  8  9 10          2  3  4  5  6  7  8
     14 15 16 17 18 19 20         11 12 13 14 15 16 17          9 10 11 12 13 14 15
     21 22 23 24 25 26 27         18 19 20 21 22 23 24         16 17 18 19 20 21 22
     28 29 30 31                  25 26 27 28 29 30            23 24 25 26 27 28 29
                                                               30 31
```

> cal 7 1991

```
          JULY 1991
      S  M  T  W  T  F  S
         1  2  3  4  5  6
      7  8  9 10 11 12 13
     14 15 16 17 18 19 20
     21 22 23 24 25 26 27
     28 29 30 31
```

BC: CALCULATOR

The format of the bc command is:

```
bc [ file ... ]
```

Bc is an interactive calculator with unlimited precision arithmetic. It takes input from any files given, then reads the standard input. Bc has many features, options, and a very powerful and rich language. For a complete list, see the online manual. To stop running bc, type the cntl-d character.

Example Usage

```
> bc
45*58.1
2614.5

i=56.78*1.1
i*1.0
62.45

67+93
160

cntl-d
```

WC: LIST NUMBER OF LINES, WORDS, AND CHARACTERS

The format of the wc command is:

```
wc [ -lwc ] [ name ... ]
```

Wc counts the number of lines, words, and characters in the named files, or in the standard input if no files are named. A word is defined as a string of characters delimited by spaces, tabs, or new lines.

Options

-l Count the number of lines

-w Count the number of words

-c Count the number of characters

If no options are specified, the number of lines, words, and characters are displayed.

Example Usage

```
> cat textfile
this is a file containing
text information

> wc textfile
      2       7      43 textfile

> wc -cw textfile
     43       7 textfile
```

SPELL: CHECK THE SPELLING OF A DOCUMENT

The format of the spell command is:

```
spell [ -v ] [ -b ] [ -x ] [ file ]
```

Spell checks every word in the file and looks them up in a spelling list. Words that are not on the spelling list nor are derivable (by applying certain inflections, prefixes, or suffixes) from words in the spelling list are printed on the standard output. If no files are named, words are collected from the standard input.

Options

With the -v option, all words not literally in the spelling list are printed, and derivations from spelling list words are flagged.

The -b option checks British spelling.

The -x option prints every plausible stem of the word with a '=' for each word.

Example Usage

```
> cat spelltext
This is a file containing a list of words. The spell checker
compares these words against the valid spellings in the file
/usr/dict/words.

> spell spelltext
spell
```

SCRIPT: RECORD TERMINAL SESSION

The format of the script command is:

```
script [ -a ] [ file ]
```

This command records everything displayed on your terminal to a file. If no file is specified, the filename typescript is used. To end a script session, type "exit".

Options

-a Append the session information to the file instead of overwriting the file.

Example Usage

```
> script
Script started, file is typescript

> date
Tue May  2 23:51:58 PDT 1989

> who
me         console May  2 21:08

> exit
Script done, file is typescript

> cat typescript
Script started on Tue May  2 23:51:50 1989
> date
Tue May  2 23:51:58 PDT 1989
> who
me         console May  2 21:08
> exit
>

script done on Tue May  2 23:52:04 1989
```

PRINTING FILES

Most Unix systems have several printers connected to the computer. To get a complete list of all the printers on your system, look at the file /etc/printcap . One printer is the default printer; a print request without specifying the printer goes to this default printer.

Printing a File

The lpr command sends a file to the printer. The format of this command is:

```
lpr [ -Pprinter ] [ filename(s) ]
```

If one or more files are listed, these are sent to the printer. The standard input is used if no files are requested. If a printer is not specified with the −P option, the output is sent to the default printer.

Listing the Files in the Printer Queue

To list all the files in the printer queue, type:

```
lpq [ -Pprinter ]
```

The print requestnumber and name of the file(s) are listed.

Removing a File from the Print Queue

To delete a print request, use:

```
lprm [ -Pprinter ] requestnumber
```

where requestnumber is the number shown by the lpq command.

GAMES

Most Unix systems come with a games directory located in /usr/games. An ls of this directory will list all the games you can play. See the online manual for a description of each of the games available.

UPTIME: HOW BUSY IS THE SYSTEM?

The uptime command shows the current time, how long the system has been up, and the load average in order for:

- 1 minute ago
- 5 minutes ago
- 15 minutes ago

The **load average** reflects the number of jobs waiting to be run. It gives you an idea of how loaded the system is—a lightly loaded workstation shows:

```
7:14pm  up 11 days, 5:21, 2 users, load average: 0.37, 0.21, 0.29
```

On one mainframe, a value of 0 to 25.0 gave excellent response, 25.0 to 45.0 was acceptable, and 45.0 to 120.0 gave such a slow response that it was better to come back at another time. On the workstation, a value of 5.0 was very slow. The acceptability of this value depends on the hardware and CPU of your system.

DU: DISK USAGE

The du command tells you how much disk space in kilobytes is used by files. The format of the du command is:

```
du [options] directoryname
```

du without any options will show you the amount of space used in each subdirectory and the total disk usage.

Options

-s Summarize. Do not show the amount of space used by each subdirectory—only the total usage.

-a All. Show the amount of space used for each file in addition to the amount used in each subdirectory and the total usage.

Usage

The major use of this command is to find unnecessary and large files in your directory. To create a file called diskusage containing a list of all your files and directories in order by the amount of disk space used, run the following command sequence:

```
du -a ~ | sort -n > ~/diskusage
```

NICE: RUN A COMMAND AT LOWER PRIORITY

The format of the nice command is:

```
nice [ -number ] command [ arguments ]
```

Nice runs the command with a lower scheduling priority. The number is any value between +1 and +10. A value of +10 is lowest priority. By default, a value of +10 is used if no priority is specified. Superusers may run a command at higher priority −1 to −10.

Commands using a large amount of the CPU should be niced. For example:

```
nice +5 du -a ~ | sort -n > ~/diskusage
```

FIND: LOCATE A FILE IN A DIRECTORY TREE

The find command is useful for searching for a file when you do not know where in the directory tree the file is located. To search for a file called tex that you know is located somewhere in the /usr/ directory, type:

```
find /usr/ -name tex -print
```

The format of the find command is:

```
find directoryname commandlist
```

Many arguments are associated with this commandlist. The most common to locate a file are:

- -name filename: Look for files with that name
- -user username: Look for files owned by that user
- -perm permission: Look for files with a certain file permission
- -atime days: Look for files accessed within a certain number of days
- -mtime days: Look for files modified within a certain number of days
- -size blocks: Files size of 512 byte blocks
- -a: And two conditions
- -o: Or two conditions

Once a file is located, you can either:

- -print: Print full pathname when the file is found
- -exec command: Execute a Unix command on that file
  The end of the command is marked with a ";". The brackets

```
{ }
```

are replaced by the name of the file.

Some symbols, such as ";", "(", ")", and "*", are needed for find, and must be put in quotes. If they are not put in double quotes, the shell interface will interpret them instead of the find command.

To list all files on the system greater than 51200 bytes:

```
find / -size +100 -print
```

Instead of printing the names of the files with print, any Unix command can be executed using the filename. To execute the command ls -lF on all files greater than 51200 bytes, use:

```
find / -size +100 -exec ls -lF "{}" ";"
```

The command between the -exec and the ";" is executed for every file found. The brackets are replaced by the filename when the command is executed.

To remove all files within your home directory with the name core:

```
find ~ -name core -exec rm "{}" ";"
```

When using or (-o) or and (-a) symbols, the conditions must be in parenthesis. To remove all files in your directory named a.out or core that have not been accessed within 10 days:

```
find ~ "(" -name a.out -o -name core ")"
                 -atime +10 -exec rm "{}" ";"
```

This command must be typed on a single line; it was split to fit on the page.

The size, atime, and mtime parameters allow for positive, negative, and absolute values. Each of these values has a different meaning:

- -atime +10: Only files that have not been accessed in 10 days
- -atime -10: Only files last accessed within 10 days
- -atime 10: Files last accessed exactly 10 days ago

The wildcard character "*" must be quoted when used in the find command. To delete all the ".bak" files in your directory, use:

```
find ~ -name "*.bak" -exec rm "{}" ";"
```

The find command uses a large amount of CPU. Within your own home directory, do not worry about the CPU usage. Avoid searching large directory trees such as /usr or the /directory. If you must search a large directory tree, lower the priority of the find command with the nice command.

SUMMARY

This chapter contained several miscellaneous commands useful to know when working on a Unix system. Some of the major commands described in this chapter were:

echo: Print a line of output
who: Show who is working on the system
script: Record terminal output to a file
lpr: Print a file
find: Find a file in the file system

EXERCISE

1. Give a one-line command to move all of your C language programs (files that end in ".c") that have been modified within the past 7 days to the directory /usr/class/cs40. These files are located in your home directory as well as various subdirectories within your home directory. □

CHAPTER 6

UNIX FILTERS

Unix relies heavily on filters to sort files and search for a certain keyword in a file. A **filter** is a command that takes some input, transforms the data, and sends this transformed data as output.

This chapter describes the following filters:

- sort: Sort information
- grep: Search for a keyword
- awk: Pattern scanning and processing
- crypt: Encrypt a message
- tee: Record data to standard output
- head: Display beginning part of a file
- tail: Display last part of a file

---

sort: SORT AND MERGE FILES

The sort command sorts information in one or more files. It allows many fields to be sorted using various keys:

sort [-bdfnrtx] [+pos1 [-pos2]] [-T directory] [name] ...

sorts the lines of all the named files together and writes the result on the standard output. If no input files are named, the standard input is sorted. By default, sort orders the entire lines starting in the first column.

Sort keys are used to specify the fields to sort. When there are multiple sort keys, later keys are compared only after all earlier keys are equal.

Options

-b	Ignore leading blanks (spaces and tabs) in fields.
-d	Only letters, digits, and blanks are significant in comparisons.
-f	Upper-, and lowercase letters are equivalent.
-n	Sort in numeric order.
-r	Sort in descending order, instead of ascending order.
-tx	'Tab character' separating fields is x.
+pos1 -pos2	Restricts a sort key to a field beginning after pos1 and ending just before pos2. Both these variables have the form m.n, where *m* tells a number of fields to skip from the beginning of the line and n tells a number of characters to skip further.
-T	The next argument is the name of a directory in which temporary files should be made.

Example Usage

This example uses a file called grocerylist. This file is a list of food items, the grocery store where they are to be purchased, and the price. The fields are separated by one or more tab characters.

```
> cat grocerylist
eggs        valuking      1.19
milk        safeway       1.97
bread       valuking       .99
lettuce     alphabeta      .59
cereal      safeway       2.45

> sort grocerylist
bread       valuking       .99
cereal      safeway       2.45
eggs        valuking      1.19
lettuce     alphabeta      .59
milk        safeway       1.97

** sort by highest to lowest price **
> sort -r +2 grocerylist
cereal      safeway       2.45
milk        safeway       1.97
eggs        valuking      1.19
bread       valuking       .99
lettuce     alphabeta      .59
```

```
** sort by grocery store then price **
> sort +1 +2 grocerylist
lettuce      alphabeta        .59
milk         safeway         1.97
cereal       safeway         2.45
bread        valuking         .99
eggs         valuking        1.19
```

---

grep: SEARCH FOR A KEYWORD

All commands in the grep family search a file or files for a pattern. The grep commands are:

```
grep [ option ] ... expression [ file ] ...
egrep [ option ] ... [ expression ] [ file ] ...
fgrep [ option ] ... [ strings ] [ file ]
```

Each line found that matches the pattern is sent to standard output. Grep patterns are limited regular expressions. Egrep patterns are full regular expressions. Fgrep patterns are fixed strings; it is the fastest of the three versions of grep because it only searches for fixed strings.

Options

- -c   Only the number of matching lines is printed.
- -i   Upper-, and lowercase letters are considered the same.
- -l   The names of files with matching lines are listed (once) separated by newlines.
- -n   Each line is preceded by the line number in the file.
- -v   All lines but those matching are printed.
- -x   Only lines matched exactly in their entirety are printed (fgrep only).

The symbols to search for a regular expression are:

- x   A single character (x) matches on that character
- \x   Matches on single character x, even if x is a special symbol
- ^   Matches beginning of the line
- $ Matches the end of the line
- .   Matches a single character
- [s]   Matches any character in the string s
- re*   Zero or more occurrences of the regular expression re

re+   One or more occurrences of the regular expression re

re?   Matches zero or one occurrence of the regular expression
             re

re1re2   Matches concatenation of regular expressions re1 and re2

re1|re2   Matches re1 or re2

(re)   Parentheses are used to enclose a regular expression.

These special symbols must be included in quotes—otherwise the
shell will interpret the special symbols instead of grep:

```
* + ? | ( ) [ ] $ \ ^
```

Example Usage

```
> cat grocerylist
eggs        valuking    1.19
milk        safeway     1.97
bread       valuking     .99
lettuce     alphabeta    .59
cereal      safeway     2.45

** show all lines that have safeway **
> fgrep safeway grocerylist
milk        safeway     1.97
cereal      safeway     2.45

** show all lines that do not have lettuce **
> fgrep -v lettuce grocerylist
eggs        valuking    1.19
milk        safeway     1.97
bread       valuking     .99
cereal      safeway     2.45

** show all occurrences of a single character, followed by **
** an a, followed by one or more l's                       **
> egrep '.al+' grocerylist
eggs        valuking    1.19
bread       valuking     .99
lettuce     alphabeta    .59
cereal      safeway     2.45

** print all occurrences of a g followed by zero or more g's **
> egrep 'gg*' grocerylist
eggs        valuking    1.19
bread       valuking     .99

** print all occurrences of gg, gggg, gggggg, . . . **
> egrep '(gg)+' grocerylist
eggs        valuking    1.19
```

```
** print all strings that  have a y or d in them **
> egrep '[yd]' grocerylist
milk      safeway    1.97
bread     valuking    .99
cereal    safeway    2.45
```

---

awk: PATTERN SCANNING AND PROCESSING

The awk command allows for complex pattern scanning and processing. For more information on awk, refer to A. V. Aho, B. W. Kernighan, P. J. Weinberger, "Awk—a pattern scanning and processing language" (Bell Laboratories, Murray Hill, N.J.) and the online manual. Awk is an entire programming language allowing complex interpreted programs. On of the most useful features of awk is the print function to reformat the output of other commands. When used in this form, the format of awk is:

```
awk [-Fcolumnseparator] '{print formatstring}'
```

where columnseparator is the character separating columns in the input and formatstring is the new format of the output. By default, the column separator is a space or a tab character. The variables $1, $2, ... are the output fields to put in the format string.

Example Usage

```
> date
Wed May 3 02:36:37 PDT 1989

> date | awk '{print $2 $3}'
May 3

> date | awk '{print $2 " " $3 " " $6}'
May 3 1989

> who
me      console May 2 21:08

> who | awk '{print $1}'
me
```

---

crypt: ENCODE AND DECODE TEXT

The format of crypt is:

```
crypt [ password ]
```

The crypt command allows confidential information to be encoded into a nonreadable form. It reads from the standard input and writes to the standard output. The password is a key that selects a particular transformation. If no password is given, crypt demands an encryption key from the terminal. When crypt is run on an encrypted file, the original text file is returned provided that the same key is used.

Example Usage

```
> cat origtext
this is a
sentence.

> crypt < origtext  > crypttext
Enter key:

> cat crypttext
b5ExG/C.]YDX(:S?QvOY

> crypt < crypttext
Enter key:
this is a
sentence.
```

---

tee: RECORD PIPE INFORMATION

The format of tee is:

```
tee [ -ia ] file
```

Information sent into the tee command is sent out in two different places: standard output and file. Tee copies its standard input to its standard output and records all the information sent in file.

Options

-i	Ignore interrupts
-a	Append output to the file rather than overwriting it

Example Usage

```
> who | tee whofile
jw     ttyp0     Apr 7 13:07

> cat whofile
jw     ttyp0     Apr 7 13:07
```

head: DISPLAY BEGINNING OF A FILE

The format of the head command is:

```
head [ -count ] [ file ... ]
```

where count is the number of lines from the top of the program to display. If no count is given, the default value is 10. When no file is specified, the input comes from standard input.

Example Usage

```
> cat grocerylist
eggs          valuking        1.19
milk          safeway         1.97
bread         valuking         .99
lettuce       alphabeta        .59
cereal        safeway         2.45

> head -2 grocerylist
eggs          valuking        1.19
milk          valuking        1.97
```

tail: DISPLAY END OF A FILE

The format of the tail command is:

```
tail +number[lbc][rf] [ file ]
```

Tail displays the end of the file to standard output—beginning at a designated place. If no file is named, the standard input is used.

The output displayed begins at distance +number from the beginning, or −number from the end of the input. Number is counted in units of lines, blocks, or characters, according to the appended option l, b or c. The default unit if none is specified is lines.

Specifying r causes tail to print lines from the end of the file in reverse order. If f option causes tail not to quit at the end of file and wait for the file to grow.

Example Usage

```
> cat grocerylist
eggs          valuking        1.19
milk          safeway         1.97
bread         valuking         .99
lettuce       alphabeta        .59
cereal        safeway         2.45
```

```
> tail -2 grocerylist
lettuce     alphabeta        .59
cereal      safeway         2.45
```

EXERCISES

1. Find all occurrences of the word "important" in any of the files in the directory /usr/local/src. Find these occurrences of "important" for any combination of upper- or lowercase letters. ☐

C H A P T E R 7

COMMUNICATION AND FILE-ARCHIVING COMMANDS

Computers running the Unix operating system are often connected to other computers. A high degree of networking exists on Unix computers. Electronic mail is sent between computers, files are transferred between computers, and bulletin-board lists run between different computers. File archiving is included in this chapter because files are often archived between different computers on a network.

The first section of this chapter describes **tar** and **compress**, which are used to archive files and compress information into a smaller file. The second section deals with networking commands that are available not only on Unix computers, but also on other operating systems. These commands allow Unix systems to communicate with systems running a variety of operating systems. These commands include **telnet** to log in to another system and **ftp** (file transport protocol). The third section discusses communication information between Unix systems. This chapter includes talk, network news service, and electronic mail. The last section discusses Unix commands that access remote resources. These commands are employed by users with accounts on several Unix systems to execute commands remotely and easily copy files between systems.

These networking commands should work on all networks. The examples in this chapter use the ARPAnet (Internet). The only differences for computers on other networks are the names of the machines.

TAR: FILE-ARCHIVE FACILITY

Tar was originally designed for archiving files to tape. It is also very useful for moving entire directory structures and storing entire directory structures in a file so they can be transferred to other systems.

A system manager should be responsible for backing up the file system on your computer. If it becomes necessary for you to backup the entire file system, please refer to Chapter 20 on managing Unix systems.

The format of the tar command is:

```
tar options directory
```

where the directory name is optional. Unlike most Unix commands, do not put a - in front of the options.

The most common tar options are:

- c: Create an archive
- x: Extract files from an archive
- p: Attempt to save file permission and ownership information
- v: Verbose mode—list each file as it is archived
- t: Test that the archive is correct
- f: Use a tar file instead of a tape

As an example of tar, the following commands will:

1. Put all your files on a tape
2. Verify they are correct, and
3. Restore the files on another system

```
cd ~
tar cv .
tar tv
<take your tape over to the other system and login to that system>
tar xv
```

Instead of using a tape, it is possible to create a tar file and copy it over to the other system. A **tar file** is a file containing the same information that would have been put on the tape. Because of the large size of tar files, make them in the /tmp directory. Never put the tar file in the same directory you are taring—this causes an infinite loop until the disk becomes full.

For example, to create a tar file of all the files in /usr/tex, do the following:

```
cd /usr/tex
tar cvpf /tmp/tex.tar .
tar tvf /tmp/tex.tar
```

After copying the file tex.tar over the network to another system, restore the files with:

```
tar xvpf /tmp/tex.tar
```

COMPRESS: **COMPRESS AND UNCOMPRESS A FILE**

The compress command allows files to be compressed to approximately one-third their original size. Sometimes tar files become quite large, and for this reason their size is reduced using the compress command. These compressed files end with a .Z suffix. For example, to compress the tex.tar file, type:

```
compress tex.tar
```

The file tex.tar.Z can now be transferred to another machine.
At the other site, type:

```
uncompress tex.tar.Z
```

to uncompress the file.

NETWORKING COMMANDS BETWEEN DIFFERENT OPERATING SYSTEMS

These commands allow Unix machines to communicate with machines running other operating systems as well as other Unix machines. These commands are **telnet** to log in to another system, **ftp** to transfer files, and **finger** to find information about someone else.

telnet: Log in to Another System

The command telnet allows you to log in to another system. The format of telnet is:

```
telnet hostname
```

The telnet command comes with many features and options. Once this command is executed, it is equivalent to connecting to a computer via a terminal connection. Provided that a hostname was specified when running telnet, the telnet session ends when exiting the other computer. For complete information, please refer to the online manual.

ftp: File Transport Protocol

FTP is the standard method for transfering files between computers on the ARPAnet. The format of the ftp command is:

```
ftp hostname
```

Once connected to the remote machine, ftp prompts for a login name and password on the remote machine. Some of the possible functions to execute from the ftp program are:

ascii	Set file transfer type to ASCII
binary	Set file transfer mode to binary
bye	End ftp session
cd remotedirectory	Change the directory on the remote machine
get filename	Copy file from remote machine to local machine
help [function]	Print informative message about the meaning of function. If no argument is given, help prints a list of known functions
lcd localdirectory	Change the directory on the local machine
ls	List files on the remote machine
mget remotefiles	Multiple get. For example mget *.c, gets all files ending with the suffix .c
mkdir remotedirectory	Make a directory on the remote machine

`mput localfiles`	Puts multiple files on the remote machine
`put localfile [remotefile]`	Puts local file on the remote machine. If remotefile is specified, the name of the file is remotefile— otherwise, the filename on the remote machine is the same as the filename on the local machine
`pwd`	Print working directory on the remote machine
`quit`	Same as bye
`recv`	Same as get
`send`	Same as put

`finger`: Look up a Person

The finger command is useful for finding out information about a person. On some systems, this command is called fing. The format of this command is:

```
finger [ username@hostname ]
```

The username may be the person's account name, last name, or first name.

The finger command lists the login name, full name, terminal name, idle time, login time, and office location and phone number (if they are known) for an individual user. If no username is given, information about all the users working on the system is shown. If no hostname is given, the local computer is used to look-up the user.

When the look-up involves an individual user, the following additional information is displayed:

1. The user's home directory and login shell
2. The plan that the person has placed in the file .plan in their home directory
3. The project on which they are working from the file .project in their home directory
4. The last time they logged into a system, and
5. If they have any unread electronic mail

Example Usage

```
> finger jw@jaguar.stanford.edu

Login name: jw                  In real life: James Wilson
```

```
Directory: /user/jw                    Shell: /bin/csh
On since Apr  8 04:19:07 on ttyp0 from Tip-MJHf.Stanfor
13 seconds Idle Time
Project: ** contents of .project file shown here **
Plan:
   ** contents of .plan file shown here **
```

From another machine at the same organization (Stanford), the full domain of the hostname is not needed:

```
finger jw@jaguar
```

COMMUNICATING INFORMATION BETWEEN UNIX SYSTEMS

This section talks about communicating information between Unix systems. All these commands are specific to the Unix operation—including talk and the network news service. The specific electronic mail systems described in this section are only available on Unix systems, although other operating systems have their own mail systems that communicate with Unix mail systems.

Talk

Communication between people on Unix systems is not limited to electronic mail. The **talk** command allows you to talk interactively with another person. The format of the talk command is:

```
talk username@hostname
```

where the @hostname is optional.

The other person is notified that you want to talk with them. Once (and if!) they want to talk with you, they do so by typing:

```
talk yourname@yourhost
```

Once a talk session is set up, one-half of your screen shows what the other person types, while you type your communication in the other half of the window. It is good manners to end the talk with a cntl-c only after both people have typed bye.

Disallowing Talk

If you do not want anyone to be able to talk with you, the command:

```
mesg n
```

will not allow talk sessions.

The y option will allow people to talk with you:

```
mesg y
```

The mesg command is normally put in your .login file.

Network News

Some sites receive Usenet newsgroups—an electronic bulletin-board system. There are a staggering number of newsgroups that can be read. To read these newsgroups, use the rn program. Just type rn to run it. Once you are in the program, the h key will give you help at any time. To post a message to any newsgroup, type Pnews (this command must be capitalized).

Electronic Mail

Many electronic mail programs exist for Berkeley Unix systems. It is impossible to discuss all of them, but four of the main mail systems are discussed here:

1. Berkeley mailer
2. MM mailer
3. MH mailer
4. GNUemacs RMAIL program

All these mail systems perform the same basic functions. They allow the user to read mail, send mail, reply to mail messages, include data from files in the mail message, forward mail messages, and list mail messages received.

Most reference books describe the Berkeley mailer. It is the oldest and most primitive of the mailers described. It has one major advantage over all the other mail systems—all Berkeley Unix systems are guaranteed to have this mailer on their systems.

Berkeley Mailer

To read your electronic mail, just type mail. Typing a ? in mail will show you all the possible options.
To send electronic mail, type:

```
mail username@hostname
```

To include a file in your mail message, type:

```
~rfilename
```

To change who you want to send the message to or the subject of a message, type:

```
~h
```

The Berkeley mailer is a line-at-a-time editor, which means that you cannote edit previous lines unless you type

```
~v
```

to enter the vi editor.

To end your message, type a cntl-d or a period on a line by itself.

MM Electronic Mail System

Type mm to run this editor. Inside this editor type read to read mail and send to send electronic mail. It is very user friendly—typing a ? at any time shows a list of the possible commands.

MH Mail Editor

A very good manual page exists on how to use the MH mail editor (man mh). To send a message, type comp. To read your messages, type inc to store your mail, show to see the first message, and then next to see the following messages.

RMAIL—GNUemacs

The RMAIL pacakge is built into GNUemacs. You can read your mail using RMAIL, go into GNUemacs and type:

```
<esc> x        and then
rmail
```

Inside of RMAIL, typing a single letter performs the following function:

- s : Send a message
- f : Forward a message
- r : Reply to a message
- p : Go to previous message
- n : Go to next message
- g : Get new mail
- j : Go to first message
- o : Output mail message to a file
- d : Delete a message
- e : Expunge deleted messages
- h : Show the headers of all the messages

After typing an s to send a message, edit your message using normal emacs control keys and escape sequences and then type:

    cntl-c cntl-s

to send the message.

Mail Notification

The biff command tells Unix if you want to be notified when electronic mail arrives. To be notified every time a mail message arrives, type:

    biff y

If you do not wish to be notified, type:

    biff n

The biff command is normally put in your .login file.

REMOTE COMMANDS

Unix provides some remote commands for a user on one system to access the resources on another system. These commands are:

1. rlogin: Remote login
2. rcp: Remote copy
3. rdist: Remote distribution
4. rsh: Remote shell

Permission to Execute

For any of these commands to work, permission must be given for the systems to communicate. This permission can be given on a system-wide basis or for just a specific account.

System-wide Permission

Some Unix systems will "trust" other Unix systems. Any account name on a trusted system can access the same account name on the local system. A list of trusted systems is put in the file /etc/hosts.equiv.

Specific-account Permission

This permission is given by creating a .rhosts file in the user's home directory. Consider the case where a user has account name john on the machines hosta and hostb and the account name jw on machine hostc. If this user wants to execute remote commands from hosta or hostc on hostb, a .rhosts file must be created in the user's home directory on hostb. This .rhosts file is a list of hostnames and account names that may execute remote commands. The .rhosts file on hostb contains:

```
hosta john
hostc jw
```

a single blank space separates the host and account name.

rlogin: Remote Login

The **rlogin** command allows a user to login to another computer. The advantage of rlogin over telnet is that an rlogoin job may be suspended. Multiple rlogin jobs can be running at the same time—allowing the user to switch between different computers.

If permission exists from /etc/hosts.equiv or a .rhosts file, the rlogin will connect the user without asking for a password. Otherwise, the user is required to type in a password.

The format of this command is:

```
rlogin hostname [-ec] [-l remote-username]
```

Without specifying a remote-username, rlogin assumes the login name is the same as the system being connected from. This is fine if john on hosta is remotely logging in to john on hostb. However, the jw account on hostc must specify a remote-username when connecting to the john account on hostb.

```
rlogin hostb -l john
```

Suspending Jobs

A ~ is the default escape character in rlogin; it causes the character following the ~ to apply to the rlogin process instead of being interpreted on the remote system. A ~ followed by a control-z will suspend the rlogin process. A ~ followed by a control-c will kill the rlogin process. A remote login session is properly ended by typing logout.

A different character from ~ can be specified with the -e option. To make + the escape character, use:

```
rlogin hostb -e+
```

`rcp:` Remote Copy

The rcp command allows files to be copied from one system to another. The rcp command has four formats. The -r option allows directories to be recursively copied.

1. `rcp [-r] remote-host:file(s) directory`
2. `rcp [-r] file(s) remote-host:directory`
3. `rcp remote-host:from-file to-file`
4. `rcp from-file remot-host:to-file`

If a file or directory is preceded by a remote-hostname, the file or directory uses the remote systems file system.

For example, John can copy his .login file from hosta to hostb with the first format on hostb.

```
rcp hosta:.login ~
```

or the second format from hosta:

```
rcp .login hostb:~
```

Unless a remote directory is an absolute pathname (beginning with a /), the directory begins at the user's home directory.

Different User Names

Consider the problem where John has different user names on different machines. To specify a different user name on the remote machine, use the following format for the remote-host:

```
hostname.username
```

John can copy his files from hostc to hostb with:

```
rcp hostc.jw:.login ~
```

from hostb, or :

```
rcp .login hostb.john:~
```

from hostc.

Permission

Unless permission is given in the /etc/hosts.equiv file or the user has a .rhosts file, the rcp command will fail. The error message `Permission`

Denied is displayed. You must also have access permission for the files and directories for rcp to work correctly.

Copying Subdirectory Trees

The -r option is used to copy entire directory systems. If any of the "files" is a directory, this entire directory tree is copied when the -r option is specified.

Assume that all users are located in the directory /usr/users and John has a subdirectory on hostb called hostabackup. John can copy every file and the directory tree structure from his hosta account to his hostb account.

From hostb, the syntax is:

```
rcp -r hosta:~ hostabackup
```

From hosta, the syntax is:

```
rcp -r ~ hostb:hostabackup
```

Using Wildcards

Wildcards symbols can be used with rcp. To copy all the C language programs (these programs end with a .c suffix) in John's home directory on hosta to hostb, use the following on hosta:

```
rcp ~/*.c hostb:
```

Wildcard symbols are interpreted on the local system unless they are quoted. To copy all these files while working on hostb, use:

```
rcp hosta:"~/*.c".
```

rdist: Remote Distribution

The rdist program keeps software consistent over several systems. It is very useful for managing several systems. One computer is designated as the software distributor, and the other computers are automatically kept up to date. The rdist command comes with many options (see the online manual for a complete list).

Most often, the command is executed as:

```
rdist -f distfile
```

A file called **distfile** contains all the control information. The following example shows how distfile uses hosta as the software distributor; hostb and hostc are supplied with the software. Both systems must have hosta in their /etc/hosts.equiv file. All the files in /usr/bin, /usr/src, and /etc are kept consistent, with the exception of a few files in /etc.

```
HOSTS = ( hostb hostc)
FILES = ( /usr/bin /usr/src /etc)
$(FILES) -> $(HOSTS)
install:
notify john@hosta ;
except /etc/passwd ;
except /etc/rc.local ;
except /etc/init ;
except /etc/fstab ;
```

John will receive an electronic mail message of errors and a list of all files that were updated.

rsh: Remote Shell

The rsh command executes a command on another system. The shell used on the remote system is the user's default shell. The format of the rsh command is:

```
rsh host [-l username] command
```

The command is executed on the remote host. If the username is different on the remote host, the "-l" option should be used. For John to execute the who command on hostb and hostc from hosta, he should use:

```
rsh hostb who
rsh hostc -l jw who
```

All relative filenames start in the home directory of the user. All the shell metacharacters (file redirection and wildcard characters) are interpreted locally unless they are quoted. The statement:

```
rsh hostb cat /etc/termcap > mytermcap
```

causes the mytermcap file to be created on the local system because the redirection symbol (>) is interpreted locally. To create the file mytermcap on hostb, use:

```
rsh hostb cat /etc/termcap ">" mytermcap
```

Commands requiring interactrive screen control (such as emacs) do not work with rsh.

SUMMARY

A Unix system with several interconnected computers requires commands to access these other computers. The most common use of remote commands are:

`mail`	Sending electronic mail to other users
`talk`	Interactive communication with another user
`finger`	Look up information about another person
`ftp`	Transfer files
`rcp`	Remote copy of files to another system
`rsh`	Remote shell access of another system

EXERCISE

1. When making a tar file, why does putting the tar file in the same directory you are taring cause an infinite loop (and eventually fills the entire disk)?   □

C H A P T E R   8

HIDDEN FILES

Hidden files are files that begin with a ".". They are control files used by a program. Some of the most common hidden files are:

- `.login`   Login initialization file
- `.cshrc`   C shell initialization file
- `.profile`   Bourne shell initialization file
- `.emacs`   Emacs initialization file
- `.newsrc`   Net news (rn) control file
- `.mailrc`   Berkeley mail initialization
- `.forward`   Forward e-mail to another address
- `.rhosts`   Allow permission for remote commands to be used
- `.plan`   File of information about you
- `.msgsrc`   File listing the system messages read

Hidden files show up with the ls command when the –a option is used.

The two most important hidden files are the **login initialization file** (.login) and the **shell initialization file** (.cshrc or .profile). The login initialization file is executed every time you log in to the system. The .login file typically sets the environment variables such as the terminal type and executes any necessary login commands.

Every time a C shell is created, the .cshrc specifies which shell variables are set and what commands are aliased.

LOGIN INITIALIZATION

This login initialization file sets the default file protection modes, search path, editor to use, format of the prompt, default e-mail notification setting; reads any system messages; and sets the terminal type. A sample .login file is shown in Figure 8.1.

```
#
# This is the default protection mode for files and directories
# that are created. Recall that a value of 033 gives a default
# protection mode of 744 (owner has read, write, and execute;
# group and others have read permission.
umask 033

#
# Each shell has a list of directory paths that are searched in
# order for any command. For example, typing "who" will cause the
# shell to look for an executable program called "who" in the
# current directory (.), then a subdirectory called bin in the home
# directory. The third and final directory searched is /usr/ucb.
#
# The directories are searched only when a pathname is not
# specified in front of the command. The string "who" would search
# through the directories, but "/usr/ucb/who" executes the program
# in the /usr/ucb directory.
#
# Before .login is run, some environment variables such as $HOME
# (home directory) are set.
set path=(.$HOME/bin /usr/ucb /usr/local/bin /usr/bin /usr/local)

#
# Some programs, such as network news, will look for a shell
# variable called "editor". This tells the program what editor to
# use for the user to type in information.
setenv EDITOR /usr/local/bin/emacs

# Set the shell prompt to be the name of the computer being
# worked on. The back'uotes execute the command and use
# the output produced by that command
set prompt="'hostname'>"

#
# Do not notify the user when electronic mail arrives.
# The user will only be notified at every login.
biff n

#
# Read any system messages that have been placed on the computer
msgs -pf
```

```
#
# Another environment variable that is set at login time is "TERM"
# This is the type of terminal used.
# To set it, use the "tset" command. The ^H is cntl-H, not
# a "^" followed by "H".
echo "Please confirm (or change) your terminal type."
loop:
# This nonobvious line does the tset.
set noglob; eval 'tset -e^H \?$TERM'
if ($TERM  == "unknown") goto loop

#
# A different "fortune cookie" message appears at every login
/usr/games/fortune
```

FIGURE 8.1

C SHELL INITIALIZATION

The commands in the .cshrc file are executed when a C shell is created. The sample .cshrc file shown in Figure 8.2 sets the number of previous commands to remember and creates many aliases.

```
#
# Set the number of previously remembered commands to 40.
# When the "history" command is typed, it will display the
# last 40 commands
set history = 40
#
# The rest of the statements are aliases.
#

# Commands aliased because they are used often. Typing an h to the
# shell executes the history command and typing g executes gnuemacs
alias h history
alias g gnuemacs

# Commands aliased because their usage is hard to remember
# The command "enscript" prints text files on a postscript
# printer in various formats. "rotateprint" is in landscape mode".
# Both commands print with a font of 8pt Courier Bold
alias rotateprint "enscript -r -f Courier Bold8"
alias smallprint "enscript -f Courier-Bold8"

# Commands aliased to perform special functions
#
# Note that once an alias is set, it may be used in a .cshrc file.
# "g" was previously aliased to be "gnuemacs".
```

```
#
# Typing editphone edits a list of phone numbers, printphone prints
# the numbers on the printer, and call displays the numbers on the
# terminal.
alias editphone  "g ~/phonelist"
alias printphone "lpr ~/phonelist"
alias call       "more ~/phonelist"

# These commands allow the user to type TOPS-20 operating
# system commands (kk, type, dir, vdir, copy, print)
# and execute the equivalent Unix commands.
alias kk exit
alias type more
alias dir ls
alias vdir "ls -lFa"
alias copy cp
alias print lpr

# A ! represents the arguments supplied to the alias. !:1 is the
# first argument. !:2 is the second argument, etc. The following
# example, when run as "mailto /etc/motd jw@polya" executes
#    "cat /etc/motd | mail jw@polya"
# This program sends the file /etc/motd in a mail message
# to jw@polya

alias mailto "cat \!:1 | mail \!:2"

#
# A backslash must be put in front of the ! because the alias
# command interprets the ! -- not the C shell.
#

# Some people prefer their prompt to show their current
# directory. Every time the directory is changed,
# the prompt needs to be changed.
#
# The command "mycd" performs the same function as the "cd"
# command. It also sets the prompt to the current directory. Note
# that the "mycd", for example, "mycd /etc" performs
#    "cd /etc ; set prompt = '/etc >'"
#
# The prompt has a relative pathname if a relative pathname is used.
# For example, a "mycd .." performs "cd .. ; set prompt = '..>'"
#
```

FIGURE 8.2

FORWARDING ELECTRONIC MAIL

Imagine the problem of having computer accounts on several different machines, but wanting to read all your mail on one system. Unix

allows you to forward your e-mail to another computer address by specifying the e-mail address in a hidden file called **.forward**. Suppose that user Barney Jones has two computer accounts: barney@uofi-a and jones@uofi-b. To have all of his e-mail on uofi-a automatically forwarded to his account on uofi-b, he should put the following .forward file in his home directory (~barney) on uofi-a:

```
jones@uofi-b
```

CREATING MAILING LISTS

The .mailrc file is used to create mail aliases. Aliases created in the .mailrc file in a user's home directory may only be used by that user. No other user can send mail to that alias. To create an alias that anyone can use, please refer to Chapter 20 on system management.

Mail aliases are used to create a mailing list, such as a list of friends or a list of employees working for you. If the .mailrc file contains:

```
alias friends alan smith zz@zap.berkeley.edu jose andy@lotus
alias employees joe moe curly
```

sending an e-mail message to the address "employees" sends the message to Joe, Moe, and Curly. Sending the message to "friends" sends it to all the friends listed in the .mailrc file.

OTHER CONTROL FILES

The rn (readnews) program uses the .newsrc file to remember what messages you have read and the newsgroups you read. Emacs uses a .emacs file for initialization purposes. Many emacs functions, including the function of the command keys, can be changed in this file.

EXERCISES

1. Alias several commands so that the interface looks similar to an IBM PC (MS-DOS). Do at least the following commands:

2.1	makedir	Make a directory
2.2	delete	Physically delete a file
2.3	type	List a file without pausing
2.4	copy	Copy a file
2.5	print	Print a file ☐

2. Create aliases so that grocery will add one or more items to a grocery list and groceryshop will print out this list.   ☐

## PART TWO

SHELL PROGRAMMING

CHAPTER 9

SHELL PROGRAMMING

Chapter 5 discussed the shell interface to Unix. It is your interface to the Unix operating system. A shell is more than just a user interface— it is an entire programming language. In this chapter, you will learn the C shell programming language.

There are several reasons for having a shell programming language, even when a programming language such as the C programming language is available for use. Some of these reasons are:

1. Shell programming is strongly designed for use with Unix commands. It is easy to use existing Unix commands for much of the programming.
2. Shell programs are machine-independent. A shell program running on one type of machine runs on any other type of machine, provided that the machines have the same Unix commands that are used in the shell program.
3. Shell programs are much more powerful for certain things than a traditional programming language. For some applications, it is much easier to write a shell program than a program in a high-level language.

There are some disadvantages with writing a shell program. Shell programs are interpreted and run much slower than a program written in a traditional programming language such as Pascal or C. In addition to performance problems, writing a traditional program with many variables and control structures is difficult in a shell program.

The chapter describes the C shell programming language and the Bourne shell programming language. The Bourne shell is included because many of the older shell programs are written in it. Most of the emphasis of this chapter is on the C shell.

C SHELL

Previous chapters used the C shell in interactive mode. It prompted you for commands to execute and interpreted special shell symbols. The shell is capable of executing commands from a file as well as prompting for commands to execute.

A shell program called dayoftheweek is shown in Figure 9.1. It prints out the day of the week by executing the command date and sending the output of the date command as input to the awk command.

```
date | awk '{print $1}'
```

FIGURE 9.1

To run this program, type csh dayoftheweek.

Automatic Shell Execution

Placing a #! at the beginning of a program automatically executes a shell. The #! must be the first line in the program, and it must start in the first column. A modified version of dayoftheweek is shown in Figure 9.2. It automatically executes the shell.

To run this program, the user needs to execute permission on the file dayoftheweek. The user only needs to type dayoftheweek because the shell is automatically executed by dayoftheweek.

```
#!/bin/csh
date | awk '{print $1}'
```

FIGURE 9.2

Shell Initialization

When a C shell is run, it looks at the .cshrc file to do all the initialization. The -f option of csh makes it run without the .cshrc initialization.

```
#!/bin/csh -f
```

Doing this improves the performance of shell programs because no initialization is performed every time the program is executed.

Whenever a blank character follows a #, the rest of the line is a comment. The dayoftheweek program can be commented as shown in Figure 9.3.

```
#!/bin/csh
#
# dayoftheweek
#
# This program prints out the date.
#
date |awk '{print $1}'# This statement prints the day
```

FIGURE 9.3

Shell Symbols

All of the special C shell symbols such as:

```
|  < >  >>  &  |&  >&
```

may be used in a shell program. Figure 9.4 shows a program called sortedwho that creates a file called wholist. This file contains the date and a sorted list of users working on the system. The program then displays this file on the screen.

```
#!/bin/csh
#
# sortedwho
#
# Prints a list of who is on the system, sorted by username
# The date is displayed at the top of the list.
date > /tmp/wholist          # put date into temporary file wholist.
who | sort >> /tmp/wholist # append sorted list of users to wholist.
more /tmp/wholist            # display the contents of wholist.
```

FIGURE 9.4

Variables

Unlike most programming languages, variables in the C shell do not need to be declared before they are used. To set a variable to some value, use:

```
set variablename = value
```

To access the value of a variable, use:

```
$variablename
```

All shell variables created using set are string variables.

The runcmd program is shown in Figure 9.5. The first line of this program sets the variable cmd to the name of a command. The next line executes the command given by the cmd variable.

```
#!/bin/csh
#
# runcmd
#
# This program executes the command stored in the variable cmd
#
set cmd = "date | awk '{print $1}' "
$cmd
```

FIGURE 9.5

Prompting for Input

It is possible for the program to prompt for input from the user. A $< reads a value from the standard input. The program runprompt in Figure 9.6 prompts the user for a command to execute.

```
#!/bin/csh
#
# runprompt
#
# This program prompts the user for a command to execute
#
echo -n "Command to execute:" # -n option says not to print a newline
set cmd = $<
$cmd
```

FIGURE 9.6

Numeric Variables

A @ assigns a string variable to the results of a mathematical equation. For example:

```
@ sum = 1 + 2
echo "$sum"
```

Arrays

Set can also be used to create a variable array. The variable cmds in Figure 9.7 is set to an array of commands to execute.

```
#!/bin/csh
#
# runcmds
#
# This program executes the commands stored in the array cmds
#
set cmds = ("date" "who" "ls")
$cmds[1]
$cmds[2]
$cmds[3]
echo "$#cmds commands were executed"
```

FIGURE 9.7

Note that:

```
$#variable-array-name
```

gives the number of elements in the array.

Arguments

It is possible to pass arguments to the shell program. The commands to execute (date, who, is) could be passed to a shell program instead of setting the variable cmds inside the program.

Consider the program runargs, which can be run in the following manner:

```
runargs date who ls
```

Date is the first argument to the program, who is the second argument, and ls is the third argument. All the arguments are stored in

```
#!/bin/csh
#
# runargs
#
# This program executes the first three
# commands passed as arguments.
#
$argv[1]
$argv[2]
$argv[3]
echo "$#argv commands were executed"
```

FIGURE 9.8

a variable array called argv before the shell executes. The contents of argv are used in the program runargs (Fig. 9.8).

Programming Constructs

The C shell has four main programming constructs:

1. foreach: For statement
2. while
3. if – then – else
4. case

Foreach construct

The format of the foreach construct is:

```
foreach variable variable-array
        <statement(s)>
end
```

The first time through the loop, variable is set to the first element in variable-array. Each time through the loop, variable is set to the next element in variable-array. Variable continues through this loop until the last element of variable-array is reached.

Consider this modified version of runargs shown in Figure 9.9. It now runs a variable number of commands instead of always having to run exactly three commands.

```
#!/bin/csh
#
# runargs
#
# This program executes whatever commands are passed as arguments
#
foreach cmd ($argv)
  $cmd
end
echo "$#argv commands were executed"
```

FIGURE 9.9

While Construct

The format of the while statement is:

```
while (condition)
        <statement(s)>
end
```

Conditions

The following symbols are valid in the condition:

- 0 : False
- 1 : True (any nonzero number means true)
- && : And
- | | : Or
- ! : Not
- < : Less than
- <= : Less than or equal to
- > : Greater than
- >= : Greater than or equal to
- == : Equals
- ! = : Not equal to
- -e filename : The file or directory filename exists
- -f filename : Filename is a file and not a directory
- -d filename : Filename is a directory and not a file
- -r filename : The user has read permission for filename
- -w filename : The user has write permission for filename
- -x filename : The user has execute permission for filename

Sample Programs

The program in Figure 9.10 performs a loop—incrementing the variable count from 1 to 10.

The program in Figure 9.11 creates an array of the powers of 2 up to 2 to the 11th power. After creating the powers, it prints the values in the array in reverse order.

```
#!/bin/csh
#
# counter
#
@ count=1
while ($count <= 10)
    echo "$count"
    @ count= $count + 1
end
```

FIGURE 9.10

```
# arrays
#
# Powers of 2 program
#
# This program prints out the powers of 2 up to 2**11
#
# must initialize array
set ary = ( 0 0 0 0 0 0 0 0 0 0 0 0 0 0 0 0 0 0 0 0 0 0 )
#
@ count=2
@ ary[1]=2
echo $ary[1]    #echo 2 (2**1)
#
# create the array
while ($count < 12)
    @ ary[$count] = $ary[$count - 1] * 2
    @ count = $count + 1
end
#
# display the values
@ count = 11
while ($count >= 1)
    echo $ary[$count]
    @ count = $count +1
end
```

FIGURE 9.11

If Construct

The format of the if statement construct is:

```
if (condition) then
  statement(s)
else if (condition) then
  statement(s)
else
  statement(s)
endif
```

The if construct can have zero or more else if statements and zero or one else statement.

One example of the if statement is a program called goodrm (Fig. 9.12). It asks whether or not you really want to remove the file. A reply of "y" moves the file to the /tmp directory and changes the permission mode so no one else may read the file.

```
#!/bin/csh -f
#
# goodrm
#
echo "Remove $argv[1]? (y/n)"
set resp = $<
if ($resp == "y") then
  chmod 700 $argv[1]
  mv $argv[1] /tmp
else
  echo "$argv[1] not removed"
endif
```

FIGURE 9.12

Case Construct

The C programming language has a case construct. The case statement should be used for speed and reliability purposes when you have many conditions to test for:

```
switch (string)
        case pattern1:
            statement(s)
            breaksw
        case pattern2:
            statement(s)
            breaksw
        default:
            statement(s)
    endsw
```

Filename Modifiers

When a variable contains a filename with a directory path in front of it, sometimes it is useful to reference only part of a filename. Filename modifiers are used to do this. These modifiers are shown in Figure 9.13.

```
set a = "programs/c/hello.c"
set b = "tmp/scratch/foobar.p"
```

$a:gt $b:gt	hello.c foobar.p
$a:ge $b:ge	c (suffix of hello) p (suffix of foobar)
$a:gr $b:gr	programs/c/hello /tmp/scratch/foobar
$a:gh $b:gh	programs/c /tmp/scratch

FIGURE 9.13

Use of Backquotes

It is possible to set a variable to the output of a Unix command by using backquotes:

```
set variable = 'command'
```

For example, the program (compileallc) compiles all the files in the current directory ending with a .c suffix. In a directory containing the files a.c and b.c, it executes:

```
cc a.c -o a
cc b.c -o b
```

This program is shown in Figure 9.14.

Debugging

To debug your program, put the statement:

```
set echo
```

inside of your shell script. After this statement is reached, the C shell will display each line of your program before it is executed.

```
#!/bin/csh
#
# compileallc
#
# This program compiles all of the C programs in a directory
#
set editfls = 'ls *.c'
foreach file ($editfls)
  cc $file -o $file:gr
end
```

FIGURE 9.14

A More Advanced Example

The shell program shown in Figure 9.15 calculates a checkbook balance. Because the C shell only allows integer numbers, all the numbers must be in cents. This program uses three files:

1. curbalance : File contains the current balance of the account
2. checklog : File contains the check number, amount, and date the check was entered in this program for each check
3. depositlog : This file contains the amount and date entered of every deposit

The program continuously displays the current balance of the account and prompts the user to do one of three things:

c. Enter check
d. Enter deposit
e. Exit

In the case where a c (Enter check) is selected, it asks the user for the check number and amount. This information is then appended to the checklog file and the balance is reduced by the check amount. When a d (Enter deposit) is selected, it asks the user for the amount, writes the amount out to the file depositlog, and adds the amount to the balance.

Notice that at the end of every transaction, the balance is written back to the file curbalance. If the system crashes when the user is in the middle of entering transaction, the files will (hopefully!) be consistent.

Recursion

True recursion is not possible in the C shell programming language. However, recursion can be simulated by having a shell program run itself.

```
#!/bin/csh
#
# Bank account balance program
#
# set balance to zero if first time program is run
if (! -f ~/curbalance) then
  echo 0 > ~/curbalance
  @ balance = 0
else
  @ balance = 'cat ~/curbalance'
endif

while(1)
  echo "Current Balance : $balance"
  echo " "
  echo "   c. Check"
  echo "   d. Deposit"
  echo "   e. Exit"
  echo -n "Input :"
  set input = $<
  if ($input == "c") then
    echo -n "Check Number : "
    set checkno = $<
    echo -n "Amount : "
    set amount = $<
    echo "$checkno $amount 'date'" >> ~/checklog
    @ balance = $balance - $amount
  else if ($input == "d") then
    echo -n "Amount : "
    set amount = $<
    echo "$amount 'date'" >> ~/depositlog
    @ balance = $balance + $amount
  else if ($input == "e") then
    exit
  else
    echo "Command Unknown! Must be (c, d, or e)"
  endif
  echo "$balance" > ~/curbalance
end
```

FIGURE 9.15

The dirsearch program shown in Figure 9.16 searches for a file in a directory tree. If no directory is initially specified, it starts searching in the current directory. The pseudocode for this program is:

```
for every file in the directory

    if the file is a subdirectory then
       run dirsearch on that subdirectory
```

```
#!/bin/csh -f
# Use -f option to greatly increase performance
# Otherwise, the .cshrc file will be initialized for every
# subdirectory.
#
# dirsearch
#
# Searches through the entire directory tree searching for the
# location of a file. When it finds a file with the name it is
# searching for, it prints out the directory of the file.
#
# Dirsearch will recursively call itself to search through
# subdirectories
#
# Format of the command list is:
#    dirsearch file [directory]

if ($#argv -- 2) then
  cd $argv[2]              # assume format of command is correct
endif

foreach file (*)
  if (-d $file) then
    dirsearch $argv[1] $file
  else if ($file == $argv[1]) then
    echo 'pwd'
  endif
end
```

FIGURE 9.16

> **else if the file is the one we are looking for then
> print out the current directory**

For the program to work properly, the program dirsearch must be located in one of the directories in the user's path. Otherwise, the dirsearch program cannot access the dirsearch program in a subdirectory. This program uses an excessive amount of CPU, so it should only be used to search for files in a small directory structure.

BOURNE SHELL

Here is a simple one-line Bourne shell program. It displays the contents of the message-of-the-day file. This is the code inside of a file that I have named message-of-the-day

```
more /etc/motd
```

To run this shell program, type:

```
sh message-of-the-day
```

Instead of saying sh message-of-the-day you can say message-of-the-day if you specify to run the Bourne shell as the first line in your program:

```
#!/bin/sh
more /etc/motd
```

The next example is a shell program to list any file where the name of the file is specified when you run the shell. The program is called list-file. To print out the message-of-the-day file using this script, you would type:

```
list-file /etc/motd
```

You can have up to nine arguments following the name of the shell program:

```
name-of-the-command argument1 argument2 ... argument9
```

To use the value of these arguments in your program use $1, $2 ... $9. For example, the program list-file would look like:

```
#!/bin/sh
more $1
```

The next example really shows the power of shell programming over a conventional programming language. Here is a program that will send a file to someone via electronic mail. The arguments to this program are the name of the file to send and where the file should be sent. This is what the mail-a-file program looks like:

```
#!/bin/sh
cat $1 | mail $2
```

Notice that any of the special shell symbols such as:

```
|, <, >, >>, and &
```

may be used.

To send the message-of-the-day file to my account, specify

```
mail-a-file /etc/motd jwilson@ferrari
```

Variables Inside of a Program

You do not need to declare variables used inside a shell program. Variables are used without being declared. Variable names must start with an alphabetic letter. To set the value of a variable name:

```
variable-name=contents-of-variable
```

For example:

```
a="Hi"
```

Caveat: Do not leave any blank spaces around either side of the = sign. Otherwise, your program will not work correctly.

To use the value of a variable, put a $— in front of the variable name. For example,

```
echo $a
```

PROMPTING FOR VALUES

What if you wanted to prompt the user to type in a value instead of passing the value as an argument? Use the read command to do this inside of your shell. The following reads in a string and then prints out the reverse of that string:

```
#!/bin/sh
read instring
cat $instring | rev
```

If Condition

Remember the danger of using the rm command? Once a file is removed, it cannot be unremoved! Here is a program called remove that will prompt you and make certain that you want to remove a file:

```
#!/bin/sh
echo "Do you really want to remove $1? (y/n)"
read resp
if test $resp = "y"
then
    echo "deleting $1"
    rm $1
else
    echo $1 not removed"
fi
```

The format of the if statement is:

```
if (condition)
then
        statement(s)
else
        statement(s)
fi
```

Note the condition of the if statement. All conditions in Bourne shell program require you to use the test command. You can test for the following conditions:

Tests on Files

-r file : File is readable

-w file : File is writable

-f file : File is not a directory

-d file : File is a directory

Tests on Strings

s1 = s2 : s1 is equal to s2

s1 != s2 : s1 is not equal to s2

s1 :   s1 is not null

-z s1 :   length of string s1 is zero

-n s1 :   length of string s1 is greater than zero

Tests on Integers

i1 -eq i2 : i1 is equal to i2

i1 -ne i2 : i1 is not equal to i2

i1 -lt i2 : i1 is less than i2

i1 -gt i2 : i1 is greater than i2

i1 -le i2 : i1 is less than or equal to i2

i1 -ge i2 : i1 is greater than or equal to i2

Multiple Test Conditions

-a : and

-o : or

For example, in the following program, the variable i is incremented from 1 to 9. The value of i is displayed every time it is incremented:

```
#!/bin/sh
i=1
while test $i -lt 10
do
      echo "$i"
      i='expr $i 1'
done
```

SUMMARY

Shell programs developed as an extension of the shell user interface. They have become an entire programming language. They use existing Unix commands for much of the programming. Shell programs are machine independent and can be easier to write than a high-level language. They are interpreted instead of compiled—resulting in slower performance than a compiled program.

Both the Bourne shell (sh) and the C shell (csh) have their own shell programming language. The Bourne shell existed before the C shell, and, traditionally, most shell programs were written in the Bourne shell language. More recently, most shell programs have been written in the C shell programming language.

EXERCISES

1. You are to write a shell script that checks every 60 seconds if a user has received any new mail within the last 60 seconds. Determine this by checking the size of the mail file. Each user has their own mail file—this mail file is located in the directory /usr/spool/mail, and the name of the file is the same as the login name of the user. *Hint:* Use wc -l to determine the size of the file. ☐

2. (*Difficult*). Write a spreadsheet calculator using a shell programming language (Bourne or C shell) to perform calculations of integer values. The format of the command is:

```
mycalc spreadsheetfile rulesfiles outputfile
```

Each rule in the rulefile is applied to the spreadsheet file. The output of applying the rules is put in the outputfile.

A spreadsheet file contains one or more lines of financial information. Each row in the spreadsheet contains four cells separated by the tab character. Each row with information will have all four cells filled with some value. A 'xxxx' means that the value of the cell will be calculated by a rule.

Two spreadsheet files to test your spreadsheet program are:

```
cars:
    1.      Car      Run1     Run2     Best
    2.      Jaguar   80       82       80
    3.      Ferrari  65       63       63
    4.      Lotus    87       87       87
    5.      Porsche  85       90       85
    6.
    7.      Avg      xxxx     xxxx     xxxx

stocks:
    1.      Name     High     Low      Close
    2.
    3.      Sun      xxxx     xxxx     xxxx
    4.      Dec      xxxx     xxxx     xxxx
    5.
    6.      37       128      0        0
    7.      38       128      0        0
    8.      38       129      0        0
    9.      39       128      0        0
```

For the stocks file, the first column of rows 6 to 9 represents the stock price of Sun Microsystems. The second column represents the stock price of Digital. The final row (row 9) is the closing price.

A rulefile contains one or more rows of rules to apply to a spreadsheet file. The rules must be applied in the order they are listed. The format of every rule in the rulefile is:

```
resultcell function fromcell tocell
```

All cell values have the format:

```
row:column
```

Your program must handle the following functions:

mean : Arithmetic mean
min : Lowest value
max : Largest value
sum : Sum of the values

These functions must work on the range of cells between (and including) fromcell and tocell.

The rules to apply to the two test examples are carrules:

```
7:2      mean     2:2      5:2
7:3      mean     2:3      5:3
7:4      mean     2:4      5:4
```

and stockrules:

```
3:2     max      6:1     9:1
3:3     min      6:1     9:1
3:3     badfunc  6:1     9:1
3:4     sum      9:1     9:1
4:2     max      6:2     9:2
4:3     min      6:2     9:2
4:4     sum      9:2     9:2
```

The mean function is not required to handle rounding—just truncate the integer value.

You should get the following output results after running these two spreadsheets:

```
Car       Run1     Run2     Best

Jaguar    80       82       80
Ferrari   65       63       63
Lotus     87       87       87
Porsche   85       90       85

Avg       79       80       78

Name      High     Low      Close

Sun       39       37       39
Dec       129      128      128

37        128      0        0
38        128      0        0
38        129      0        0
39        128      0        0
```

You are not required to check for any error conditions except those explicitly stated in this assignment. Errors you do not have to check for include invalid cell formats, cell widths other than four cells, and column and row positions out of range.

Hint: Use awk -F: {print $1} and awk -F: {print $2} to separate row and column numbers for a cell position (i.e., 7:3). Make use of awk to separate column position. Use head and tail to get a certain row in a file. □

## PART THREE

APPLICATIONS PROGRAMMING IN THE C PROGRAMMING LANGUAGE WITH UNIX

MAKEFILES: SOFTWARE ENGINEERING

The make facility of Unix is useful for maintaining computer software. The make facility is the solution to two important software problems: program maintenance and software installation.

PROGRAM MAINTENANCE

One of the largest costs of a software product during its lifetime is the maintenance cost of fixing bugs and adding features to the software. This maintenance cost can be as high as 80 percent of the total cost of the software.

Software goes through the life cycle shown in Figure 10.1. All software projects go through this life cycle. Sometimes the same person will perform all the activities, but they are separate functions that must be performed in this order.

The **System analysis** phase determines what is needed. This analysis is done by talking with the customer who is purchasing the software, or just having an idea for a new software product.

System design diagrams how this software can be written. Menu screens are designed. Modules are drawn to show how the various parts of a system are interrelated.

The next three stages are a loop of program **coding, compiling the software**, and **testing**. If the software does not compile correctly, the code is fixed. Testing is performed after it compiles correctly. Any problems while testing result in the code being modified until the problems are fixed. Often, code is not written all at once; a small part of it is written at a time and tested before the next part is written.

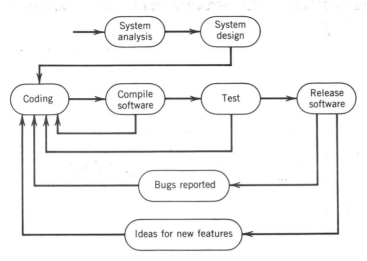

FIGURE 10.1

Eventually, the software is completed and customers start using it. Sometimes, they will find additional bugs and have ideas for new features to put in the software.

For program maintenance, the make facility compiles the software. It verifies that all the software programs affected by a coding change are compiled. This next section on software consistency shows the importance of this verification.

SOFTWARE CONSISTENCY

Definitions

This chapter uses several definitions you should be familiar with:

- **Software package**: A collection of one or more related programs
- **Source program**: A program written in C or some other high-level language
- **Object program**: Created by compiling a source program
- **Executable program**: Program that can be executed. Created by linking together one or more object programs
- **Include file**: List of definitions used by a source program. These definitions are included when the source program is compiled.

Physical Implementation of Makefiles

The make command reads a file called **makefile** to determine how to keep software consistent or how to install a software package. These makefiles are important because they provide for good software engineering by keeping executable files consistent with the source files. They also make it easy for any user to install software on a system.

Multiple source and include files may be used to create a single executable program. Makefiles make certain that any changes made in a source program or include file will cause the executable file to be recompiled.

Importance of Software Consistency

Before describing how makefiles work, it is important to stress why it is necessary to have a facility such as makefiles to keep software consistent. Consider the following example using an include file called number.h and two C programs called mainpgm.c and returnnum.c. Number.h defines a constant, and returnnum.c has a function that returns this value. The main program prints out the value returned by the function.

Figures 10.2 through 10.4 give the code for these programs:

```
/* number.h */
#define USE_NUM 10
```

FIGURE 10.2

```
/* mainpgm.c */
main()
  {
    int return_num();
    printf("%d\n",return_num());
  }
```

FIGURE 10.3

```
/* returnnum.c */
#include "number.h"
int return_num()
  {
    return USE_NUM;
  }
```

FIGURE 10.4

In this example, the source file returnnum.c is compiled to create the object file returnnum.o. The source program mainpgm.c is compiled to create mainpgm.o. The object programs returnnum.o and mainpgm.o are then linked together to create the executable file a.out. Executing a.out causes the number 10 to print out.

The following sequence of commands shows how to create the object programs, link them together, and run the executable program:

```
cc -c mainpgm.c
cc -c returnnum.c
cc mainpgm.o returnnum.o
a.out
```

Consider what happenes when number.h is changed from:

```
#define USE_NUM 10
```

to

```
#define USE_NUM 12
```

Running a.out still prints the number 10. To get it to print out 12, returnnum.c must first be recompiled and then the files returnnum.o and mainpgm.o must be linked together again. To guarantee all the changes to the source files and include files will be a part of a.out, some dependencies must be created. The file creation date of a.out must be more recent than returnnum.o and mainpgm.o. If a.out is older than either of the source files, it must be recreated. The program returnnum.o must be up to date with respect to number.h and returnnum.c.

Dependency Graph

A graph of these dependencies can be drawn. The dependency graph for this software package is shown in Figure 10.5.

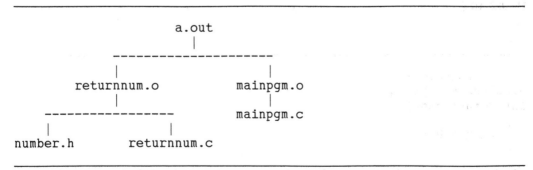

FIGURE 10.5

All the necessary Unix commands to do this are stored in a makefile. A makefile tells make what commands to perform. By default, the make command uses a file in the current directory called Makefile. If this file does not exist, the make command looks for a file called Makefile in the current directory.

The format of the make command is:

```
make [-f file] [target]
```

where the target is the executable or object file you want to make. If a file is specified with the -f option, this file is used instead of the makefile.

The makefile describes these dependencies and the make command looks at the makefile to determine how to keep the software up to date based on the dependencies.

The format of a makefile is:

```
target: dependency(ies)
<tab>    command1
<tab>    command2
     ...
```

The dependency graphs for psi and young are shown in Figure 10.6.

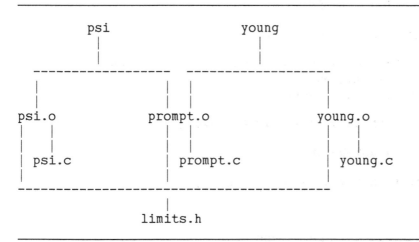

FIGURE 10.6

Source Code

The source code for this package is shown in the programs limits.h, prompt.c, psi.c, and young.c. The code for these programs is shown in Figures 10.7 through 10.10. The file limits.h just defines constants

```
/* limits.h */
#define MAXFORCE          100000.0
#define MAXWIDTH         2.0
#define MAXDEPTH         0.5
#define MAXSTRAIN      3.0
#define MAXLOAD          (MAXFORCE / (MAXWIDTH * MAXDEPTH))
#define TRUE             1
#define FALSE            0
```

FIGURE 10.7

```
/* prompt.c */
#include "limits.h"
float promptReal(promptString,max)
    char *promptString;
    float max;
  {

    float valueToReturn;
    int valueWasSpecified;

    valueWasSpecified = FALSE;

    while (valueWasSpecified == FALSE)
      {
        printf("What is the value of %s\n",promptString);
        scanf("%f",&valueToReturn);
        if (valueToReturn > max)
          {
            printf("Maximum value is %f\n",max);
          }
        else if (valueToReturn < 0.0)
          {
            printf("Minimum value is 0.0\n");
          }
        else
          {
            valueWasSpecified = TRUE;
          }
      }
    return valueToReturn;
  }
```

FIGURE 10.8

```
/* psi.c */
#include "../limits.h"

extern float promptReal();

main()
  {
    float force,width,depth;

    force = promptReal("Force (lbs.)",MAXFORCE);
    width = promptReal("Width (in.)",MAXWIDTH);
    depth = promptReal("Depth (in.)",MAXDEPTH);

    printf("Pounds per square inch (PSI) is %f\n",(force / (width *
depth)));
  }
```

FIGURE 10.9

```
/* young.c */
#include "../limits.h"

extern float promptReal();

main()
  {
    float load1,load2,strain1,strain2;
    load1 = promptReal("First Load (PSI)",MAXLOAD);
    load2 = promptReal("Second Load (PSI)",MAXLOAD);

    strain1 = promptReal("First Strain",MAXSTRAIN);
    strain2 = promptReal("Second Strain",MAXSTRAIN);

    printf("Young's Modulus is %f\n",(load2 - load1) /
           (strain2 - strain1));
  }
```

FIGURE 10.10

used in the program. The function in prompt.c prompts for a valid floating-point value and returns this value. The files psi.c and young.c just compute the psi and youngs modulus equations.

Output Produced

The two executable programs (psi and young) produce the output shown in Figure 10.11.

```
>psi
What is the value of Force (lbs.)
1000
What is the value of Width (in.)
.05
What is the value of Depth (in.)
.02
Pounds per square inch (PSI) is 999999.937500

>psi
What is the Value of Force (lbs.)
1000
What is the value of Width (in.)
.5
What is the value of Depth (in.)
.02
Pounds per square inch (PSI) is 100000.000000

>young
What is the value of First Load (PSI)
20000
What is the value of Second Load (PSI)
50000
What is the value of First Strain
.02
What is the value of Second Strain
.025
Young's Modulus is 5999999.000000
```

FIGURE 10.11

Makefiles

Three targets are defined in the makefiles:

1. `all`: Compile all the necessary software
2. `install`: Install the software on the system
3. `clean`: Remove all the unnecessary object and executable programs

The makefile in the main directory controls the execution of the makefiles in both subdirectories. These three makefiles are shown in Figures 10.12 through 10.14.

```
# makefile in mechpackage directory
all:
        cd young; make all
        cd psi; make all

install:
        cd young; make install
        cd psi; make install

clean:
        rm -f *.o
        cd young; make clean
        cd psi; make clean
```

FIGURE 10.12

```
# makefile in psi subdirectory
INSTALLDIR= /MyDisk/Homes/me/bin
ALL= psi

all: $(ALL)

# The source and object files for prompt.c
# are located in the main directory. Therefore
# the target ../prompt.o is necessary.
#
../prompt.o: ../prompt.c ../limits.h
        cc -c ../prompt.c -o ../prompt.o

psi.o: psi.c ../limits.h
        cc -c psi.c

psi: ../prompt.o psi.o
        cc ../prompt.o psi.o -o psi

install:
        make all
        cp $(ALL) $(INSTALLDIR)

clean:
        rm -f $(ALL)
        rm -f *.o
```

FIGURE 10.13

```
# makefile in young subdirectory
INSTALLDIR= /MyDisk/Homes/me/bin
ALL= young

all: $(ALL)

../prompt.o: ../prompt.c ../limits.h
        cc -c ../prompt.c -o ../prompt.o

young.o: young.c ../limits.h
        cc -c young.c

young: ../prompt.o young.o
        cc ../prompt.o young.o -o young

install:
        make all
        cp $(ALL) $(INSTALLDIR)

clean:
        rm -f $(ALL)
        rm -f *.o
```

FIGURE 10.14

Dependencies in the Makefile

Cleaning Up the Directory

Makefiles often define a clean dependency. A make clean removes all unnecessary files such as object and executable files. In this example, the makefile in the mechpackage directory (the main makefile) removes all the object files and performs a make clean in the subdirectories. Both the subdirectory makefiles delete all the object and executable files. The output of executing a make clean is shown in Figure 10.15.

Often a make clean is performed after a make install to remove unnecessary files. The -f option for the rm command is necessary to

```
>make clean
rm -f *.o
cd young; make clean
rm -f young
rm -f *.o
cd psi; make clean
rm -f psi
rm -f *.o
```

FIGURE 10.15

prevent the makefile from crashing if it tries to remove a file that does not exist.

Making All the Executables

After performing a make clean, none of the object or executable files exist. A make all needs to recreate all these files. The main makefile performs a make all in the young and the psi subdirectories. In the young subdirectory, the object files prompt.o and young.o must be created before the executable file young may be created. In the psi subdirectory, the executable file psi requires psi.o to be created. The object file prompt.o is already up to date because it was created by the makefile in the young subdirectory. As no rules exist in the makefile for creating young.o and psi.o, the default dependency is used—an object file (psi.o, young.o) must be up to date with respect to the source program (psi.c, young.c). The output of executing a make all is shown in Figure 10.16.

```
> make all
cd young; make all
cc -c ../prompt.c -o ../prompt.o
cc -c young.c
cc ../prompt.o young.o -o young
cd psi; make all
cc -c psi.c
cc ../prompt.o psi.o -o psi
```

FIGURE 10.16

SOFTWARE INSTALLATION

Performing a make install will copy psi and young to the installation directory called /MyDisk/Homes/me/bin. The output of executing a make install is shown in Figure 10.17.

```
> make install
cd young; make install
make all
cp young /MyDisk/Homes/me/bin
cd psi; make install
make all
cp psi /MyDisk/Homes/me/bin
```

FIGURE 10.17

Note that this software package will perform a make all to verify all the software is up to date before installing the software.

SUMMARY

Makefiles are important for software engineering. They provide an easy way to compile all the necessary software—verifying that all the necessary software is compiled. They also provide an easy mechanism to install software.

Makefiles contain targets, dependencies, and instructions to make the target. Targets are what you want to make. Dependencies specify which files must be up to date before the target can be made. The instructions define how to make the target.

EXERCISES

1. A software package consists of the source programs main.c, sub1.c, sub2.c, sub3.c. The object files from these four source files are linked together to create an executable file called mainipgm. The source files main.c and sub2.c include the file constants.h. The files main.c and sub1.c include the file limits.h.

   a. Draw the dependency graph for this software package.

   b. Create a makefile for this software package.   □

C H A P T E R   11

HANDLING ERRORS

The previous chapters of this book can be completed without knowing the C programming language. This chapter is the start of describing Unix system calls, and a working knowledge of the C programming language is assumed. Error handling is used throughout the rest of this book.

This chapter describes three kinds of errors when writing a C program in the Unix environment:

1. Compile errors
2. Run-time errors
3. Errors when making Unix system calls

COMPILE ERRORS

Most compile errors are self-explanatory and will give you the line number and reason for the error. There are three common problems that you may come across: excessive number of errors, displaying compile errors, and going to the correct line number of your program.

When you get an excessive number of compile errors, quite often these errors are caused by the first couple of syntax errors listed in your program. I have seen students look over pages of compile errors—all of which were caused by the first couple of syntax errors. A solution to this problem is to edit the first few errors in your program and recompile the program.

All compiler errors are sent to standard error, not standard output. To redirect your compile errors to a file, use the ">&" symbol, not ">":

```
cc yourpgm.c >& errorfile
```

To pipe the compile errors to the more command, use:

```
cc yourpgm.c |& more
```

Once you know the line number where a syntax error occurred, how do you find this line number in your program? With emacs, the command sequence:

```
control-u line-number control-n
```

will move you down to the correct line, provided you start at the top of the program. To move to the top of your program, use:

```
escape-key <
```

In vi, the command:

```
line-numberG
```

will move you to a certain line number.

RUN-TIME ERRORS

After the program compiles correctly, it may contain one or more run-time errors that need to be fixed. There are two main methods of debugging the run-time errors in a program. They are the **ctrace** and **dbx** facilities.

Ctrace Facility

The ctrace facility takes your C program and automatically inserts printf statements after every line in your program. The new program created with all these printf statements is then compiled. The statement being executed and any variables that changed are displayed. This ctrace facility is not available on all Unix systems.

Consider the program dividebyzero.c that causes a divide-by-zero error. It first performs the calculation 1000/1 and then 1000/0. This second calculation causes a floating-point exception.

```
main()
  {
    int i,j;

    for (i=1;i>=0;i--)
      {
        j = 1000 / i;
        printf("%d\n",j);
      }
  }
```

To create, compile, and execute this new program with the ctrace facility, use:

```
ctrace dividebyzero.c > newdividebyzero.c
cc newdividebyzero.c
```

The output of this program is:

```
1 main()
5    for (i=1;i>=0;i--)
     /* i == 1 */
6      {
7        j = 1000 / i;
         /* i == 1 */
         /* j == 1000 */
8        printf("%d\n",j);
         /* j == 1000 */
1000

9      }
5    for (i=1;i>=0;i--)
     /* i == 0 */
6      {
7        j = 1000 / i;
         /* i == 0 */ Floating exception (core dumped)
```

dbx Debugging Facility

The program dbx is a run-time debugging facility, which can be used to debug C, Fortran, and Pascal programs. It provides the ability to:

1. Stop under certain conditions (line number reached; function called; or variable changed)
2. Display the contents of variables, structures, and source-code listings
3. Step through a program line-by-line

When debugging a C program using dbx, all the source programs must be compiled with the -g option:

```
cc -g dividebyzero.c
```

To run dbx, type:

```
dbx executable
```

If no executable filename is specified, the file a.out is assumed.

Running a Program from dbx

To execute a program in dbx, use:

```
run [argument(s)]
```

If you normally run your program with some options or file redirection symbols, they should be specified with the run command. This command will execute a program until a run-time error occurs or a breakpoint is reached.

To stop debugging a program, type:

```
quit
```

Listing the Source Program

The list command lists the contents of the source program:

`list`	List the next ten lines of the program
`list all`	List the entire program
`list first, last`	List all lines between first and last

Trace Facility

The trace command is used to watch when certain functions are called, line numbers are reached, or a certain variable changes:

`trace function =`	Notify when function is called
`trace variable =`	Notify when value of variable changes
`trace line-number =`	Notify when line-number is reached
`trace =`	Display every line number and variable change

Displaying the Value of Variables

Use print to display the value of a variable or expression:

```
print variable
print expression
```

Setting Breakpoints

Breakpoint can be set in the program so that it stops execution under certain conditions:

stop variable	Stop if variable changes
stop at line-number	Stop at line-number
stop in function	Stop if function called
cont	Continue execution after stopped
step	Execute one source line
next	Run until next source line has finished execution
status	List all traces and breakpoints
delete number	Delete trace or breakpoint

The difference between step and next occurs on a procedure call. The step command stops at the beginning of the called procedure; the next command stops after the procedure is executed.

Sample dbx Usage

The comments (* *) describe what is going on in this dbx session and are not a part of DBX.

```
> dbx
dbx version 2.0 of 2/26/88 10:01.
Type 'help' for help.
enter object filename (default is 'a.out'):
reading symbolic information ...

(dbx) run
1000
Floating-point exception (integer divide by zero trap) in main at
line 7
    7           j = 1000 / i;
(dbx) print i
0
(dbx) print 1000 / i
error: division by 0

(dbx) list
    1    main()
    2        {
    3           int i,j;
    4
    5           for (i=1;i>=0;i--)
    6               {
    7                  j = 1000 / i;
    8                  printf("%d\n",j);
    9               }
   10        }
```

```
(* trace program execution *)
(dbx) trace
[1] trace

(* stop every time line 7 is executed *)
(dbx) stop at 7
[2] stop at 7

(* display breakpoints and trace parameters *)
(dbx) status
[1] trace
[2] stop at 7

(dbx) run

entering function main
trace:      2    {
trace:      5        for (i=1;i>=0;i--)
[2] stopped in main at line 7
    7             j = 1000 / i;

(* step through line by line *)
(dbx) step
trace:      8            printf("%d\n",j);
stopped in main at line 8
    8             printf("%d\n",j);

(dbx) step
1000
trace:      9        }
stopped in main at line 9
    9         }

(dbx) status
[1] trace
[2] stop at 7

(* delete second breakpoint *)
(dbx) delete 2

(dbx) status
[1] trace

(dbx) quit
```

ERRORS IN SYSTEM CALLS

System calls are procedure calls to the underlying operating system, and are necessary to access system resources such as the file system. Many of the Unix system calls return a value of zero if they work correctly and -1 if some error occurs. The procedure perror can be called to print why an error occurred; it prints the reason for the last error that occurred in a system call. The format of perror is:

```
void perror (errorstring)
     char *errorstring;
```

The errorstring is displayed along with the reason for the error to provide additional debugging information:

```
errorstring: reason-for-error
```

Sample Use of perror

The following example shows a program trying to create 100 pipes. The pipe system command returns a value of -1 in case of an error. Do not worry about what the program is trying to do (this is covered in later chapters), just notice that the call to perror causes the appropriate message to be displayed. The program is:

```
main()
  {
    int  pipefd[2];
    int i;
    for (i=0;i<100;i++)
       {
         if (pipe(pipefd)  == -1)
            {
              perror("error creating pipe");
              exit();
            }
       }
  }
```

The output is:

```
error creating pipe:  Too many open files
```

SUMMARY

Errors may occur when compiling a program, running a program, or making a Unix system call in a program. Utilities such as dbx and ctrace allow debugging of a program while it is executing. The function perror prints out the reason why an error occurred when making a system call.

CHAPTER 12

FILE-SYSTEM CALLS

Unix originated as an experiment in file-system design. Chapter 2 described how to use commands to access the file system. This chapter describes Unix system calls that would be made from a C program to access the file system. The Unix file-system calls are divided into three categories, which also define the three sections of this chapter:

1. File system access: how to open, close, read, and write a file
2. Directory access: how to make, delete, and access directories
3. File status information: size of files, protection modes, file ownership

FILE SYSTEM COMMANDS

Each program has a **file descriptor table**. This is an array of pointers to open files and hardware devices. (In Unix, the hardware devices are accessed through the file system, just like a file.)

When a program is started, it has three open file descriptors; standard input, standard output, and standard error. The standard input is usually the keyboard; the standard output and standard error are usually the terminal console. Figure 12.1 shows a file descriptor table.

There are five system commands to access files:

1. Open: Open a file
2. Close: Close a file

```
                      ------
standard input   0 | -------> keyboard
                      ------
standard output  1 | -------> console
                      ------
standard error   2 | -------> console
                      ------
                 3 |free|
                      ------
                 4 |free|
                      ------

                   ..
```

FIGURE 12.1

3. Read: Read information from a file
4. Write: Write information to a file
5. Lseek: Allow random access of information in a file

When a program executes the system call open, the file is opened and the table is searched for the first free file descriptor. This file descriptor is changed to point to the open file, and the open system call returns the file descriptor number (array position in the file descriptor table). All the other file operations (read, write, close, and lseek) reference a file by this file descriptor number.

When using any of the file system calls, the file file.h must be included in your program. This file is located in /usr/include/sys/, so you must put the following in your program:

```
#include <sys/file.h>
```

Open

The format of the open command is:

```
int open (filename,accessmode,protectionmode)
        char *filename;
        int accessmode;
        int protectionmode;
```

Access Mode

The following access modes are defined when you include file.h.

- O_RDONLY : Open file for read only
- O_WRONLY : Open file for write only
- O_RDWR : File can be both read and written at the same time

- O_APPEND : Like O_WRONLY except that the output is appended to the file
- O_CREAT : Create the file if it does not exist
- O_TRUNC : Truncate a file size back to zero. This is very important when overwriting an existing file. If the new information takes up less bytes than the original file size, failure to specify O_TRUNC causes the final part of old information to remain in the file.

These access modes can be or'ed together to combine functionality. For example, to create a file and open it for write only, use:

```
( O_CREAT | O_WRONLY )
```

The open call will open the file and return an integer value called the **file descriptor number**. A value of -1 will be returned in case of an error.

Protection Mode

The protection mode is ignored unless the file is being created by the open statement. When a file is being created, the protection mode is based on the mode of the chmod command. Each protection has a number value associated with it:

- 4 : Read permission
- 2 : Write permission
- 1 : Execute permission

For example, read and write permission is a value of $(4 + 2) = 6$. File protection is given for:

1. User
2. Group the user belongs to
3. Anyone on the system

To give read and write permission to the owner of a file, give read permission to anyone in the user's group, but do not allow anyone else on the system to touch this file; use the file protection number 0640. The leading zero is necessary because the file protection is an octal number.

Close

The format of close is:

```
int close (filedescriptor)
        int filedescriptor;
```

The filedescriptor is the file descriptor number. Close will return a value of −1 in case of an error.

Read

Read will read information from a file. The format of read is:

```
int read(filedescriptor, buffer, numberofbytes)
    int filedescriptor;
    char *buffer;
    int numberofbytes;
```

The buffer is a pointer to an array of character. The numberofbytes tells the maximum number of characters (bytes) available in this array. The value returned from read is the actual number of bytes read into the buffer. The end-of-file is determined when read returns a value of zero for the number of bytes read.

Write

Write puts the information from a buffer into a file:

```
int write(filedescriptor, buffer, numberofbytes)
    int filedescriptor;
    char *buffer;
    int numberofbytes;
```

The value −1 is returned if some error occurs when writing the buffer data. Otherwise, the value returned is the number of bytes written to the file.

Lseek : Direct File Access

The read and write system calls will sequentially read and write information in a file. A file pointer is set to the beginning of a file when the file is open. Every read (or write) advances the pointer in the file by the number of bytes specified. The location of this file pointer can be changed by using the lseek system call. The format of lseek is:

```
int lseek (filedescriptor, offset, fromwhere)
        int filedescriptor;
        long offset;
        int fromwhere;
```

The value of fromwhere is defined in file.h. It is:

- L_SET : Start from the beginning of the file
- L_INCR : Start from the current location of the file pointer
- L_XIND : Start from the current end of the file

Lseek returns the position of the file pointer if it succeeds; otherwise, it returns a -1 on failure.

Lseek can be used in connection with read and write to provide for direct access to any record in addition to sequential access of the records in a file.

A few example uses of lseek are:

1. `lseek(fd, 0, L_SET)` : Set file pointer to beginning of the file
2. `lseek(fd, -18, L_XIND)` : Set pointer 18 bytes before end of the file.
3. `lseek(fd, 20, L_INCR)` : Advance pointer by 20 bytes.

Example Use of the File-System Calls

The following program, shown in Figure 12.2, copies the file /etc/motd into a file called `mymotd` in the current directory. The variable fdin is the file descriptor of the input file (/etc/motd) and the variable fdout is the file descriptor of the output file (mymotd).

Standard C I/O Routines

The C language has many file operations defined in the language. These operations include getchar, putchar, fopen, fclose, fscanf, fprintf, fgets. For compatibility, all these operations defined for the C language may be used in Unix programs. These C file operations are defined on top of the Unix I/O primitives. For example, fopen uses the open Unix system call.

All the C language file operations will work, provided that the file `stdio.h` is included in any program using these routines. For more information, please refer to a textbook on the C programming language.

DIRECTORY SYSTEM CALLS

Unix is based on a hierarchical file system with many directories. Sometimes it is useful to be able to move between different directories when your program is running or to create and delete directories.

This section describes the different Unix system calls, which are used to manipulate directories and default file protection modes. They are:

- `getwd`: Get working directory
- `chdir`: Change working directory
- `mkdir`: Make a directory
- `rmdir`: Remove a directory
- `umask`: Set default file protection mode

```
/* copy.c */
#define BUFSIZE 512
#define PMODE   0644
        /* permission mode rw user - r group and others */
        /* The 0 is necessary in front of the 0644      */
        /* because it must be an octal number.          */
#include <stdio.h>
#include <sys/file.h>

main()
    {
        char buf[BUFSIZE];
        int    n;
        int    fdin;       /*file descriptors */
        int    fdout;

        fdin = open("/etc/motd",O_RDONLY,0);
        fdout = open("mymotd",(O_WRONLY|O_CREAT|O_TRUNC),PMODE);

        if ((fdin == -1) || (fdout == -1))
    {
        printf("error opening files\n");
        exit();
    }
 while ((n = read(fdin, buf, BUFSIZE)) > 0)
    /* n is number of bytes read */
    {
        write(fdout, buf, n);
    }

 close(fdin);
 close(fdout);
}
```

FIGURE 12.2

getwd: Get Working Directory

The getwd system call:

```
    char *getwd(pathname);
            char *pathname
```

returns the name of the current directory in pathname. The full pathname of the directory is given. The function getwd returns a pointer
to the location of the variable pathname.

The following example shows how getwd can be used:

```
main()
  {
    char pathname[100];
    getwd(pathname);
    printf("The current working directory is %s\n",pathname);
  }
```

chdir : Change Current Working Directory

The chdir system call changes the current working directory your program is executing in. The format of chdir is:

```
int chdir(pathname)
    char *pathname;
```

Pathname can be an absolute or relative pathname. A value of −1 is returned if the pathname does not exist or the program does not have access permission on the directory referenced by pathname.

mkdir: Make a Directory

The mkdir system call works just like the Unix command mkdir with the exception that you also specify the protection mode when you make the directory. The system call is defined as:

```
int mkdir(pathname, mode)
    char *pathname;
    int mode;
```

where pathname is the same as described above for chdir and mode is the file protection mode described earlier in the chapter. A value of −1 is returned if the directory could not be created.

rmdir: Remove a Directory

rmdir removes a directory. It will not work correctly if the directory is not completely empty:

```
int rmdir(pathname)
    char *pathname;
```

A value of −1 is returned if it does not work correctly.

umask: **Default File Protection Mode**

The umask system call allows the program to change the default file (and directory) protection mode when a file is created. The umask is the opposite value of what you want your protection mode to be.

Subtract the following numbers from each digit of 0777 to get the umask mode:

- 4: Read permission
- 2: Write permission
- 1: Execute permission

Read and write permission is a value of $7 - (4 + 2) = 1$. To set your default so that you can read, write, and execute, and not allow anyone else to touch your files and directories, use the value 0077.

The file protection is the negation of the umask value and the mode of the file or directory. If the mode is 644 and the umask is 077, the file is created with mode 600:

```
file protection = creation mode & (~ umask)
                =    644  &  (~ 077)
                =    644  &   700
                =    600
```

The format of the umask system call is:

```
int umask(newmask)
    int newmask;
```

ACCESSING DIRECTORY INFORMATION

A directory contains quite a bit of information about subdirectories and files in the directory. The ls command uses this information when listing files. To read this information, your program must include the file /usr/include/sys/dir.h.

This include file defines the data type DIR. It is the definition of an entry in a directory. It also defines the structure type direct:

```
struct   direct {
            u_long  d_ino;                  /* inode number of entry */
            u_short d_reclen;               /* length of this record */
            u_short d_namlen;               /* length of string
            char    d_name[MAXNAMLEN + 1];
};
```

There are four main calls to access directory information. Only the first three are necessary to list the names of the files and subdirectories.

The fourth call is needed to find out additional information, such as the file protection mode:

1. opendir
2. readdir
3. closedir
4. stat

opendir

The format of the opendir system call is:

```
DIR *opendir(directoryname)
    char *directoryname;
```

readdir

Each call to readdir reads information about the next file or subdirectory within a directory:

```
struct direct *readdir(directorypointer)
            DIR *directorypointer;
```

closedir

When finished reading directory information, use:

```
void closedir(directorypointer)
        DIR *directorypointer;
```

Example of ls

The program shown in Figure 12.3 uses opendir, readdir, and closedir. It produces the same output as the ls command with the -a option.

STAT: GET ADDITIONAL INFORMATION ABOUT A FILE

In the previous example, we could only print out the name of a file. The stat system call is given a direct pointer and returns the following information about a file or subdirectory:

```
struct stat {
    dev_t     st_dev;        /* device inode resides on */
    ino_t     st_ino;        /* this inode's number */
    u_short   st_mode;       /* protection */
    short     st_nlink;      /* number or hard links to the file */
    short     st_uid;        /* user-id of owner */
```

```
    short       st_gid;          /* group-id of owner */
    dev_t       st_rdev;         /* the device type, */
    off_t       st_size;         /* total size of file */
    time_t      st_atime;        /* file last access time */
    int         st_spare1;
    time_t      st_mtime;        /* file last modify time */
    int         st_spare2;
    time_t      st_ctime;        /* file last status change time */
    int         st_spare3;
    long        st_blksize;      /* optimal blocksize */
    long        st_blocks;       /* actual number of blocks allocated */
    long        st_spare4[2];
};
```

The format of the stat system call is:

```
int stat(filename, buffer)
        char *filename;
        truct stat *buffer;
```

```
/* Produces the same output as the Unix command "ls -a" */

#include <sys/types.h>
#include <sys/dir.h>

main(argc,argv)
  int argc;
  char *argv[];
{
  DIR *dp;
  struct direct *dentry;

  if (argc > 1)
    dp = opendir(argv[1]);
  else
    dp = opendir(".");

  dentry = readdir(dp);
  while (dentry != NULL)
    {
      printf("%s\n",dentry->d_name);
      dentry = readdir(dp);
    }
  closedir(dp);
}
```

FIGURE 12.3

All the structure information is put into the buffer. Be certain that a proper filename is specified—otherwise, garbage information will appear in the buffer. The example in Figure 12.4 works because dentry is a subdirectory or file in the current directory. If this is not the case, concatenate the full pathname before the name dentry->d_name.

This modified version of the previous program shows the use of stat to get the file protection mode. The file /usr/include/sys/stat.h must be included in the program.

```
#include <sys/types.h>
#include <sys/dir.h>
#include <sys/stat.h>

main(argc,argv)
  int argc;
  char *argv[];
{
  DIR *dp;
  struct direct *dentry;
  struct stat buffer;

  if (argc > 1)
    dp = opendir(argv[1]);
  else
    dp = opendir(".");

  dentry = readdir(dp);
  while (dentry != NULL)
    {
      if (stat(dentry->d_name, &buffer) == -1)
        {
          perror("incorrect stat access");
          exit();
        }
      else
        {
          printf("%o %s\n", (buffer.st_mode & 0777),
            dentry->d_name);
          dentry = readdir(dp);
        }
    }
  closedir(dp);
}
```

FIGURE 12.4

SUMMARY

This chapter described the Unix file system. The system calls to access file-system information are divided into three categories:

1. File system access: How to open, close, read, and write a file
2. Directory access: How to make, delete, and access directories
3. File status information: Size of files, protection modes, file ownership

The system calls open, close, read, and write allow input and output to a file. The system calls getwd, chdir, mkdir, and rmdir allow access, removal, and creation of directories. The umask system call changes the default file protection mode. The third type of file system call involves file status information. This information is accessed with opendir, readdir, stat, and closedir.

EXERCISES

1. Create a C program that works exactly like the ls command called myls. It should handle the following options: -a, -1, -F, -R. See the online manual for more information. The system calls system and exec that are described in later chapters may not be used in your program. □

2. Create a C program called mycp that copies files in the same manner as the cp command. The program mycp should work in the same manner and handle the same options as the cp command. □

C H A P T E R   13

FORKS: CREATING MULTIPLE PROCESSES

DAEMONS

The **daemon** is an important concept in Unix. A daemon is a process that waits for a user to request some action, and then performs the request. For example, the ftp (file transport protocol) daemon waits around until some user requests that a file be transferred to the system. However, the ftp daemon must always be ready to receive requests to transfer files at the same time as it is transferring files.

To solve this problem, most daemon processes make a copy of themselves and create an identical process. The original process (called the **parent process**) continues to wait for requests, while the new process (called the **child process**) handles the request.

Basics

A daemon process uses the fork system call to create an identical copy of itself. Figure 13.1 shows the use of the fork command.

When this program is run, it first prints out "Hello". Then, the fork causes an identical copy of this process to be created. Both the parent and the child process print out "I am a process". The output from running this program is shown here:

```
1. main ()
2.   {
3.     printf("Hello\n");
4.     fork();
5.     printf(" I am a process\n");
6.   }
```

FIGURE 13.1

```
Hello
   I am a process
   I am a process
```

The step-by-step execution of this program (assuming the parent finishes before the child process) is that the process executes line three of the program, printing out the string "Hello". Executing the fork system call on line four causes an exact copy of the process to be made, as shown in Figure 13.2.

After the fork is executed, both processes are ready to execute line five. The parent prints out the string "I am a process" and, later on, the child process prints out the same string.

The parent and the child process are completely independent after the fork. There is no guarantee which process will first print "I am a process".

This example shows that the child process does not start at the beginning of the program—it starts right after the fork just like the parent.

When a fork is performed, everything in the parent process is copied to the child process. The contents of the variables, the code, and the file descriptor table are all copied to the new child process. Once the child process has been created, the processes' variable spaces for the child and parent are completely separate; changing the value of a variable in one process will not affect the value of the same variable in the other process.

```
1. main()                                  main()
2.   {                                        {
3.     printf("Hello\n");                       printf("Hello\n");
4.     fork();                                  fork();
5. -> printf(" I am a process\n");   -> printf(" I am a process\n");
6.   }                                        }
   Parent process                     Child process
```

FIGURE 13.2

DETERMINING THE PARENT AND CHILD PROCESSES

If the parent and child processes are completely identical, how does a process determine whether it is the parent or the child? The **fork call** is a function that not only causes an identical process to be created, but also returns a value to each process telling whether it is a parent or a child. Fork returns a value of zero to the child process and returns the process id of the child process to the parent. In the case of an error, fork returns a value of −1. Consider Figure 13.3, which tests the value returned by fork.

Assuming that the parent process finishes before the child process, the output from executing this program is:

```
Hello
   I am the parent process
   I am the child process
```

MULTIPLE FORKS

A program is not limited to performing a single fork; a process can have as many forks as desired (up to the maximum number of processes allowed for a single user).

```
main()
  {
    int pid;

    printf("Hello\n");
    pid = fork();
    if (pid == -1)
      {
        perror("bad fork");
        exit();
      }
    if (pid == 0)
      {
        printf("  I am the child process\n");
      }
    else
      {
        printf("  I am the parent process\n");
      }
  }
```

FIGURE 13.3

```
1. main()
2.   {
3.     fork();
4.     fork();
5.     fork();
6.     fork();
7.     printf("Hello\n");
8.   }
```

FIGURE 13.4

The program in Figure 13.4 prints "Hello" 16 times.

At the first fork on line three, the parent process creates a child process; the parent and child processes are now running on the system. Both these processes are now ready to execute line four of the program. Executing the second fork on line four creates two more processes. Four processes are now running. Eight processes are created by line five of the program. Each of these eight processes creates a child process by the fork on line six of the program. This program creates a total of 16 processes—each process printing the string "Hello".

This is not an efficient method of printing "Hello" 16 times. Every fork call is "expensive" because it takes a lot of system processing to create a new process.

Wait

Consider the case where you want to guarantee that the child process executes before the parent process. Shared variables do not exist in Berkeley Unix,* so you cannot perform synchronization by using a shared variable.

The **wait** system call must be used for synchronization. It causes the parent process to wait until one of its child processes exits. The wait call returns the process id of the child process, in case you have multiple child processes and want to wait for a certain one to complete. A status variable must be passed to wait. This status variable gives additional (but usually not necessary) information about the child process such as whether or not it terminated normally.

The program in Figure 13.5 guarantees that the child process prints "Hello" before the parent process prints "World":

*Some derivatives of Berkeley Unix have shared memory, such as Digital's Ultrix and Sun's operating system.

```
#include <sys/wait.h>
main()
  {
    union wait status;
    int pid;

    pid = fork();
    if (pid == -1)
      {
        perror("bad fork");
        exit();
      }
    if (pid == 0)
      {
        printf("Hello ");
      }
    else
      { /* parent process */
        wait(&status);
        printf(" World\n");
      }
  }
```

FIGURE 13.5

SUMMARY

A process makes an identical copy of itself by using the fork system call. The original process is called the parent process and the new process is called the child process. The wait system call causes the parent to wait for a child process to complete. Otherwise, the two processes are completely independent and the order of execution is not guaranteed.

EXERCISES

1. You are to create a program that creates four processes. The original process creates two children processes and then prints out "parent". The children processes print "child1" and "child2", respectively. The first child process creates a child process that prints out "grandchild". □

2. Same problem as the first exercise, except that the output must be
guaranteed to print out in the following order:

```
2.1 grandchild
2.2 child1
2.3 child2
2.4 parent  □
```

EXECUTING COMMANDS FROM A PROGRAM

The **exec** system call overlays a process run space with another program. Everything except the file descriptor table is overwritten. Exec's are often used in combination with forks to create communicating processes running different programs.

Many versions of exec exist. The most common are execl, execv, execlp, and execvp. Exec calls ending in "p" use your C shell search path when executing the command. Execl and execv require the entire search path of the command to be given.

SYSTEM

A call to the Unix operating system routine called **system** is the easiest way to use exec. System forks off a child process execute the command given to it and waits for the command to finish executing.

The format of system is:

```
system (string)
    char *string
```

For example, a C program to execute date and then ls looks like:

```
main()
  {
    system("date");
    system("ls");
  }
```

System can also handle any of the special shell symbols:

```
main()
  {
    system("cat /etc/motd | sort > sortedmotd");
  }
```

EXEC'S

System actually performs one or more calls to an exec to execute the commands. The command to execute is passed to exec, which executes the command. Exec causes the code of the executing process to be replaced by the code for the command. Everything is replaced except the file descriptor table. Once exec is called, there is no way to return to the original code in the program.

System creates a child process to execute the command, and the parent process waits for the child process to complete. This allows your program to continue execution after executing the command. The pseudocode for System looks something like:

```
#include <sys/wait.h>
system(string)
char *string;
{
  union wait status;
  int pid;

  pid = fork();

  if (pid == -1)
    {
      perror("bad fork");
      exit();
    }

  if (pid == 0)
    execute the command given by (string);
  else
    wait(&status);
}
```

Execlp

Many different versions of exec are available for use ("man exec" describes all of them). The two most common execs used are **execlp**, when you know the number of arguments ahead of time, and **execvp**, when you do not know the number of arguments.

The execlp system call is given the binary program to execute, the name that the program is known as to the system (argv[0]), and zero or more arguments. The format of the execlp command is:

```
execlp(program-to-run, program name, [argument(s)], (char *) 0);
```

For example, to run the ls command with the "−l" option:

```
main()
  {
    execlp("/bin/ls","ls","-l",(char *) 0);
    printf("Error occurred trying to execute ls\n")
  }
```

The printf statement will never be reached unless ls is not executable or does not exist. The program-to-run is the binary code to execute. The program name is the name by which the process is known. The variable argv[0] in C programs is the program name. If the program-to-run is not an absolute pathname, the user's C shell search path will be searched.

Execvp

The format of the execvp system call is:

```
execvp(program-to-run, address-of-argument-list);
```

For example, the following program takes the arguments that are passed to it and executes the command. Running the program with:

```
a.out date                  executes "date",
a.out ls -l -F -a           executes "ls -l -F -a", and
a.out |nger jwilson@polya   executes "|nger jwilson@polya"
```

The code for this program is:

```
main(argc, argv)
  int     argc;
  char    *argv[];
  {
    execvp(argv[1], &argv[1]);
  }
```

Execl and Execv

Execl and execv work in the same manner as execlp and execvp, except that the user's C shell search path is not checked. The entire pathname must be given for the program-to-run.

SUMMARY

An exec system call overlays a process run space with the executable code of another program. The original executable program is replaced with a new program. The original file descriptor table is used with this new executable program.

EXERCISES

1. Given what you know about forks and execs, create a program in the C language that executes all the commands given as arguments. For example,

   ```
   a.out who ls
   ```

   will first execute the who command and then execute the ls command. This program with the following arguments:

   ```
   a.out ls cd who
   ```

   executes ls, cd, and then who.
   Do not use system in your solution.   □

2. Using forks and execs, create a program in the C language that executes all the commands with each command separated by the "+" symbol. For example,

   ```
   a.out cd /tmp + who
   ```

   will first execute cd /tmp and then execute the who command. This program with the following arguments:

   ```
   a.out ls /usr + cd /tmp + ls -a
   ```

   executes ls /usr, cd /tmp, and then ls −a.
   Once again, do not use system in your solution.   □

CHAPTER 15

PIPES

A **pipe** is a means of communication between two processes. One process writes information into a pipe while a second process reads this information out of the pipe. This information is read in the same order that it is written.

This chapter describes the pipe system call to create pipes from inside a C program. The csh shell uses this pipe system call when it sees the "|" symbol.

In the csh a pipe connects the standard output of one command to the standard input of another command. For example:

```
who | sort
cat /etc/motd | sort | rev | more
```

Pipes can only be used between processes that originally start out as a single process and used fork to create multiple copies of the process. One process writes bytes into a pipe (just as if it were writing to a file) while the other process reads bytes from the pipe (just as if it were reading from a file).

Pipes use the same primitives as the file system. Read, write, and close work exactly the same way for pipes as they do for files. The only difference is opening a pipe. Opening a file creates a single file descriptor, whereas opening a pipe creates two file descriptors—one for each end of the pipe.

USING PIPES

The system call to create a pipe and return the two descriptors is:

```
int pipe(fileids)
    int fileids[2];
```

Pipe returns a value of -1 in case of an error, otherwise it returns a value of 0. The variable array fileids contains the file descriptor number of the read end of the pipe and the write end of the pipe. Fileids[0] is the file descriptor number of the read end, and fileids[1] is the file descriptor number of the write end.

The file descriptor table before and after the call to pipe (assuming no other files have been opened) is shown in Figure 15.1.

Recall that the file descriptors stdin, stdout, and stderr are defined before a program begins execution.

The variable fileids[0] gives the file descriptor number of the read end of a pipe, and fileids[1] gives the file descriptor of the write end of a pipe.

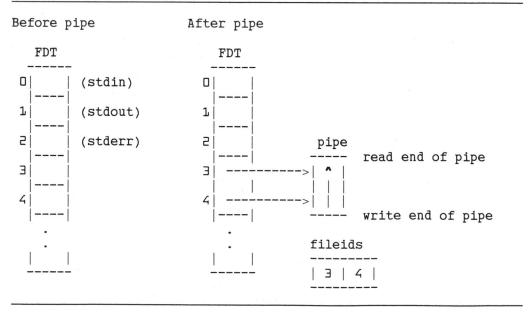

FIGURE 15.1

In Figure 15.2, a child process reads from the pipe and the parent process writes to the pipe. Note that the pipe must be created before the processes fork (because both processes must have file descriptors to the pipe). Each pipe provides only one-way communication; information flows from one process into another. For this reason, it is important that only one open file descriptor exists on each end of the pipe; the parent and the child must close the unused ends of the pipe. Another important reason for closing unused ends of pipes is that the process reading from the pipe blocks when making the read system call unless the pipe contains enough information to fill the reader's buffer or the end-of-file character is sent. This end-of-file character is sent through the pipe when every file descriptor to the write end of the pipe is closed. Therefore, a process reading from the pipe and forgetting to close the write end of the pipe will never be notified of the "end-of-file".

The main steps of Figure 15.2 are:

1. Create the pipe
2. Fork to create two processes
3. Close unused ends of the pipe
4. Parent writes to the pipe
5. Parent closes write end pipe
6. Child reads from the pipe
7. Child closes read end of pipe

A diagram of the file descriptor from executing each step of Figure 15.2 is shown here:

After pipe is created

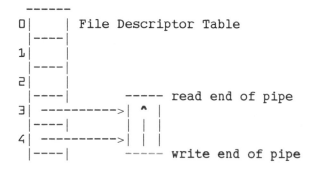

After fork

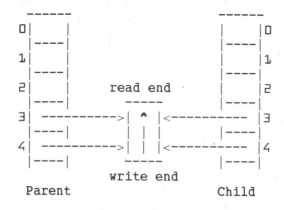

close unused ends of pipe

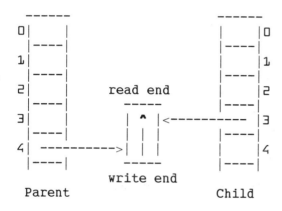

Parent sends message "hello"

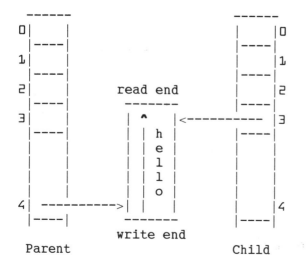

Parent closes pipe

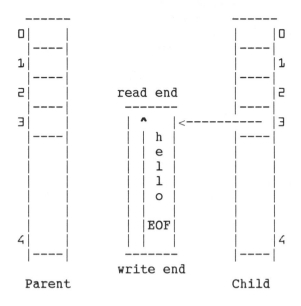

Child reads from pipe

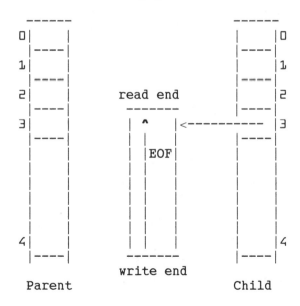

Child closes read end of pipe
(pipe goes away when both ends are closed)

```
      ------                        ------
   0|      |                      |      |0
    |----|                        |----|
   1|      |                      |      |1
    |----|                        |----|
   2|      |                      |      |2
    |----|                        |----|
   3|      |                      |      |3
    |----|                        |----|
   4|      |                      |      |4
    |----|                        |----|
    Parent                        Child
```

```c
main()
  {
    char buf[80];
    int  pipefd[2];
    int  pid;

    if (pipe(pipefd) == -1)
      {
        perror("Error creating pipe");
        exit();
      }

    pid = fork();
    if (pid == -1)
      {
        perror("bad fork");
        exit();
      }

    if (pid == 0)
      { /* child process */
        close(pipefd[1]);
        read(pipefd[0],buf,80);
        printf("%s\n",buf);
        close(pipefd[0]);
      }
    else
      { /* parent process */
        close(pipefd[0]);
        write(pipefd[1],"hello",5);
        close(pipefd[1]);
      }

  }
```

FIGURE 15.2

CONCURRENCY

The previous example showed little advantage to using a pipe rather than a file. The information could have been written to a file by one process and read from the file by another process. In the previous example, the child process waits for the parent process to finish because the read operation blocks until EOF is sent (parent closes pipe). The parent never sent enough information to fill the child's buffer (80 characters). If the parent sends 80 characters of information, the child process can read the information from the pipe and continue running before the parent closes the pipe.

Concurrency means that more than one process may be running at the same time. Pipes allow concurrency because the parent can write information into the pipe and the child can read information from the pipe at the same time. There is no guarantee when the processes will run or in what sequence of operation; they are two separate processes. The only timing guarantee is that the process reading from a pipe will block if not enough information exists in the pipe to fill its buffer and the "end-of-file" has not been sent. As soon as enough information becomes available to fill the buffer, the reading process can continue executing.

Figure 15.3 is the program of a two-process copy program. One process opens the file specified as the first argument (argv[1]) and puts the information into the pipe. The second process reads the information from the pipe and puts it into a new file; the name of the second file is the second argument (argv[2]).

Note that the child process is writing information into the pipe 80 bytes at a time, while the parent process reads information 5 bytes at a time. All the information is read by the parent process; it has to perform 16 (80 bytes of information/5 bytes per read) reads from the pipe for every 80 bytes the child process writes to the pipe.

The child process opens the file and writes the information into the pipe. The parent process reads from the pipe and writes the information into the new file. The parent and child processes execute concurrently.

STANDARD INPUT AND OUTPUT

When two Unix commands are connected with a pipe in the C shell, the standard output of one process is piped to the standard input of another process. The standard input must be changed to be the read end of the pipe, and the standard output must be changed to be the

```
#include<file.h>

#define PMODE    0644

main(argc,argv)
  int    argc;
  char *argv[];
  {
    char  buf[80];
    int   n;
    int   fdin;
    int   fdout;
    int   pipefd[2];
    int   pid;

    if (pipe(pipefd) == -1)
      {
        perror("Pipe creation error");
        exit();
      }

    pid = fork();
    if (pid == -1)
      {
        perror("bad fork");
        exit();
      }
    if (pid == 0)
      { /* child */
        close(pipefd[0]);
        fdin = open(argv[1],0);

        /* read from input file and write to pipe */
        while ((n = read(fdin, buf, 80)) > 0)
          {
           write(pipefd[1], buf, n);
          }
        close(pipefd[1]);
        close(fdin);
      }

    else
      { /* parent */
        close(pipefd[1]);
        fdout = open(argv[2],(O_WRONLY|O_CREAT|O_TRUNC),PMODE);
        /* read from pipe and write to output file */
        while ((n = read(pipefd[0], buf, 5)) > 0)
          {
            write(fdout, buf, n);
          }
        close(pipefd[0]);
        close(fdout);
      }
  }
```

FIGURE 15.3

write end of the pipe. The method to change both these is the dup2 system call. The format of dup2 is:

```
int dup2(origfd, dupedfd)
      int origfd;
      int dupedfd;
```

The file descriptor in dupedfd is mapped to the same file, device, or pipe in origfd. To make standard output the write end of pipe, use:

```
dup2(fileids[1],1);
```

To make standard input the read end of the pipe, do:

```
dup2(fileids[0],0);
```

The program of Figure 15.4 executes the equivalent of the C shell command "who | sort". The child process executes "who", while the parent process executes "sort". The six steps in this program are:

1. Create the pipe
2. Fork the process (creating two processes)
3. Each process closes the end of the pipe it is not using
4. The child process makes standard output the write end of the pipe and the parent process makes standard input the read end of the pipe
5. Close the original end of the duplicated file descriptor
6. Use execlp to run the appropriate Unix command

The file descriptors and pipes from executing the program in Figure 15.4 are shown here.

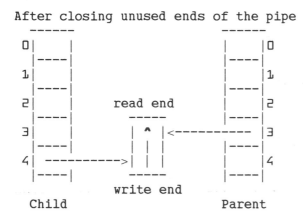

Duplicate file descriptors

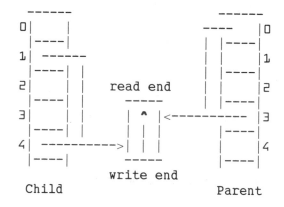

Close original ends of the pipe

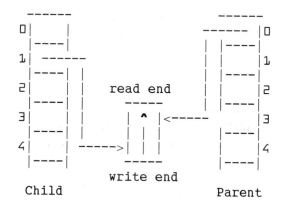

When execlp is used

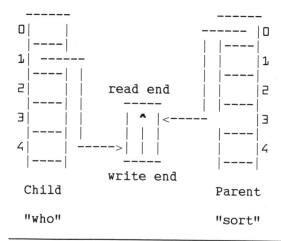

FIGURE 15.4

The code for the program of Figure 15.4 is:

```
/* who | sort    example */


main()
  {
    int fileids[2];
    int pid;

    /* 1. create the pipe */
    if (pipe(fileids) == -1)
      {
        perror("error");
        exit();
    pid == fork();
    if (pid == -1)
      {
        perror("bad fork");
        exit();
      }

    /* 2. fork the process */
    if (pid == 0)
      { /* child */
        /* 3. Close unused end */
        close(fileids[0]);
        /* 4. Duplicate file descriptor */
        dup2(fileids[1],1);
        /* 5. Close original end */
        close(fileids[1]);
        /* 6. Use execlp to run the command */
        execlp("who","who",(char *) 0);
      }
    else
      { /* parent */
        /* 3. Close unused end */
        close(fileids[1]);
        /* 4. Duplicate file descriptor */
        dup2(fileids[0],0);
        /* 5. Close original end */
        close(fileids[0]);
        /* 6. Use execlp to run the command */
        execlp("sort","sort",(char *) 0);
      }
  }
```

MULTIPLE PIPES

The previous program shows how to connect two Unix commands
through a single pipe, but what if you want a variable number of com-

mands; each one piped to the next one? The program in Figure 15.5 (pipe3) takes a variable number of arguments and pipes the standard output of each command to the standard input of the next command, and creates a child process for each command. After creating all the children processes, the parent reads from standard input and writes to standard output.

```
Arguments pipe3 is run with        Equivalent C shell syntax
  pipe3 who sort                       who | sort
  pipe3 who rev sort more              who | rev | sort | more
```

Executing **pipe3 who sort** (Figure 15.5) causes the following file descriptors and pipes:

---

commandnum = 1; before dup2

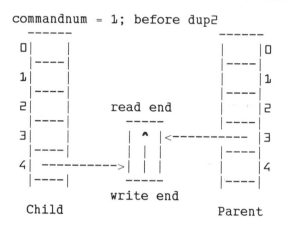

commandnum = 1; before child executes "who"

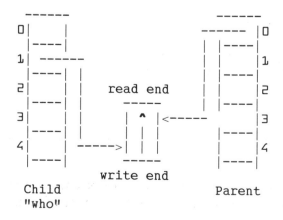

commandnum = 2; before dup2

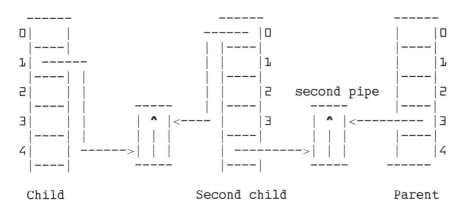

Child   Second child   Parent

commandnum = 2; before second child executes "sort".

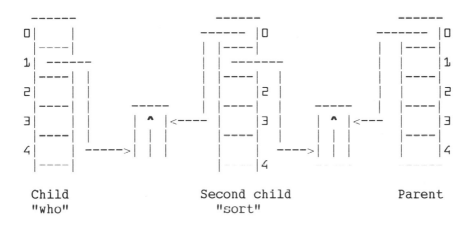

Child   Second child   Parent
"who"   "sort"

```
/* pipe3.c (Figure 15.5) */

main(argc,argv)
  int argc;
  char *argv[];
    {
      int    fileids[2];
      char   buffer[80];
      int    bytesread;
      int    commandnum;
      int    pid;

      for (commandnum = 1; commandnum < argc; commandnum++)
        {
          if (pipe(fileids) == -1)
            {
              perror("error creating pipe");
              exit();
            }
```

```
            pid = fork();
            if (pid == -1)
              {
                perror("bad error");
                exit();
              }
            if (fork() == 0)
              { /* child */
                close(fileids[0]);
                dup2(fileids[1],1);
                close(fileids[1]);
                execlp(*(argv + commandnum),
                          *(argv + commandnum),(char *) 0);
                perror("error in execlp");
                exit();
              }
            else
              { /* parent */
                close(fileids[1]);
                dup2(fileids[0],0);
                close(fileids[0]);
              }
          }

     while ((bytesread = read(0,buffer,80)) > 0)
        {
          write(1,buffer,bytesread);
        }
  }
```

Figure 15.5

SUMMARY

Pipes are "infinitely" large byte-stream buffering devices, allowing two processes to communicate. One process writes information into the pipe, while the other process reads information out of the pipe. These two processes must start out as one process and use fork to create the other process.

EXERCISES

1. It is possible to use two pipes and create two-way communication between two processes (In practice, this is not done because sockets are available for use. They are described in Chapter 17). Create a program where the parent process reads the name of a language

from standard input: French, Spanish, or English. The parent sends the name of the language to the child process via a pipe. The child determines the proper word for "good-bye": Au revoir (French), Adios (Spanish), or Good-bye (English) and sends this word to the parent using another pipe. The parent prints out the word. □

2. Write a program where the child process executes the command specified in argv[1]. The output of the child process is sent to a parent process. The parent process is a filter that converts every " " (space) to a ".". □

C H A P T E R   16

SIGNALS: INTERRUPTS

Signals are events that may happen while a program is executing. There are two general categories of signals—**interrupts** and **exceptions**. Interrupts are usually generated by the programmer, such as typing a cntl-z to stop a job or a cntl-c to terminate a job. Exceptions are errors that occur while the program is running, such as a floating-point overflow or a pointer out of range.

Each signal has a default action. The default action for a cntl-c interrupt is to terminate the program, and the default action for cntl-z is to stop the job. Instead of taking this default action, a program can ignore a certain signal or specify some software action to take when a signal occurs.

The most common signal types in Berkeley Unix are:

Number	Signal	Default action	Meaning
1	SIGHUP	Exit	Lost connection to terminal (hangup)
2	SIGINT	Exit	Interrupt (cntl-c) in shell
3	SIGQUIT	Core dumped	Quit
4	SIGILL	Core dumped	Illegal signal
5	SIGTRAP	Core dumped	Trace interrupt (used by debuggers such as dbx)
8	SIGFTP	Core dumped	Floating-point exception
9	SIGKILL	Exit	Terminate execution (CANNOT be caught or ignored)

10	SIGBUS	Core dumped	Bus error (memory protection violation)
11	SIGSEGV	Core dumped	Memory segmentation violation
14	SIGALRM	Exit	Alarm clock timed out
15	SIGTERM	Exit	Terminate execution (CAN be caught or ignored)
17	SIGSTP	Stop job	Stop signal (from process)
18	SIGTSTP	Stop job	Stop signal (from keyboard)

A **core dump** means that the contents of the program—code, variables, and state—are put into a file called core before the program exits.

All these signals are defined in the include file signal.h. This file must be included in any program that uses signals:

```
#include <signal.h>
```

HANDLER ROUTINES

Handler routines are "called" when a signal occurs. A signal causes the handler to be immediately executed. When the handler is finished, execution of the program continues where it left off.

USING SIGNALS

The signal command tells which handler routine to execute when a certain signal occurs. It is used to ignore signals and to change the action performed when a signal occurs. The format of the signal command is:

```
old-signal-handler = signal (signal-type,new-signal-handler);
    int (* old-signal-handler)();
    int (* new-signal-handler)();
    int signal-type;
```

Normally, the old-signal-handler is ignored. It just specifies the previous signal handler. Once you specify a handler routine with signal, that routine will be used until you specify a different handler routine. A common misconception is that signal waits for a signal to occur; it only tells which handler to execute in case a signal occurs.

DEFAULTS AND IGNORING SIGNALS

Every signal has a default action. Specify the default action by using:

```
signal(signal-type, SIG_DFL);
```

SIGKILL is the only signal that cannot be ignored. All others can be ignored by using:

```
signal(signal-type, SIG_IGN);
```

Be careful when ignoring signals. Once your program executes:

```
signal(SIGINT,SIG_IGN);
```

it cannot be exited with cntl-c.

SLEEP: WAIT A CERTAIN NUMBER OF SECONDS

The Unix system call sleep causes your program to stop execution for a certain number of seconds. The number of seconds to sleep is passed as an argument to the system call:

```
void sleep (number-of-seconds)
     int number-of-seconds;
```

This call uses the alarm interrupt SIGALRM to delay the program; alarm interrupts are covered later in this chapter. After the number-of-seconds are reached, the program is made available to run; there is no guarantee that the program will execute as soon as it is available to run.

The system call usleep works in the same manner as sleep, except that the program waits a certain number of milliseconds:

```
void usleep (number-of-milliseconds)
     int number-of-milliseconds;
```

IGNORING AND RESTORING DEFAULT ACTIONS

The program in Figure 16.1 shows how to ignore signals and restore the default action of a signal. It uses the sleep system call, causing the process to sleep for a certain number of seconds. By ignoring SIGINT

```
#include <signal.h>

main()
  {
    int i;

    signal(SIGINT,SIG_IGN);
    for (i=0;i<15;i++)
      {
        printf("Cannot type control-c to exit\n");
        sleep(1);
      }

    signal(SIGINT,SIG_DFL);
    printf("\nType control-c to exit\n");
    sleep(10);
  }
```

FIGURE 16.1

signals (cntl-c), it cannot be interrupted for a total of 15 seconds (15 iterations, each waiting 1 second). After 15 seconds, it restores the default handler and cntl-c will interrupt the program.

CREATING HANDLER ROUTINES

Handler routines are procedures that have the following restrictions:

1. They may not have any parameters.
2. They must be declared in the code before they are referenced.*
   Failure to do so will result in a compiler error.

The program in Figure 16.2 shows how to solve the problem of a user accidentally typing cntl-c and exiting the program. The handler routine confirm catches the SIGINT signal and asks users whether or not they really want to exit.

KILL

The system call **kill** allows a process to send any signal to a process. Sending a SIGTERM or SIGKILL signal to another process causes that process to exit, provided:

---

*A forward declaration may be used.

```
#include <signal.h>
#include <stdio.h>

int confirm()
  {
    char yes_or_no;
    char carriage_return;

    printf("\nDo you really want to exit? (Y/N)");
    scanf("%c%c",&yes_or_no,&carriage_return);
    printf("%c\n",yes_or_no);
    if ((yes_or_no == 'y') || (yes_or_no == 'Y'))
      {
        exit();
      }
  }


main()
  {
    int i;

    signal(SIGINT,confirm);
    for(i=1;i<=20;i++)
      {
        printf("Going through loop number %d\n",i);
        sleep(1);
      }
  }
```

FIGURE 16.2

1. The processes are owned by the same user, or the process killing another process is owned by the root user.
2. The process must know the process id of the process it wants to kill.

The format of kill is:

```
kill (process-id, signal-id);
     int process-id;
     int signal-id;
```

process-id is the process you want to kill. The signal id is the signal you want to send to a process. This signal is usually SIGTERM (request to terminate) or SIGKILL (force process to terminate).

```
#include <signal.h>
#include <sys/wait.h>

int pid;
int myalarm()
  {
     kill (pid,SIGKILL);
     printf("Goodbye kid\n");
  }

main();
  {
     union wait status;
     pid = fork();
     if (pid == -1)
       {
          perror("bad fork");
          exit();
       }

     if (pid == 0)
       {
          for(;;)
            {
               printf("I am a child process -- wild and free \n");
               sleep(1);
            }
       }
     else
       {
          signal(SIGALRM,myalarm);
          alarm(5);
          wait(&status);
       }
  }
```

FIGURE 16.3

ALARM

Every Unix program has a built-in alarm clock. The timer can be set and a handler routine executed when it goes off. The SIGALRM signal is sent when the alarm clock goes off, causing the SIGALRM handler routine to execute. The format of the command to set the alarm is:

```
alarm (number-of-seconds);
      int number-of-seconds;
```

The ualarm system call sets an alarm for a certain number of milliseconds.

```
ualarm (number-of-milliseconds);
       int number-of-milliseconds;
```

A process will not stop executing when it makes an alarm system call; it returns immediately from the call without delaying and continues execution.

Any call to sleep resets the alarm clock, so it is important not to use sleep if you also use alarm. The program in Figure 16.3 works because the child process is using sleep while the parent process uses alarm. The child process just runs in an infinite loop. The parent process sets an alarm to go off in 5 seconds and waits for the child process to complete. After the 5 seconds are up without the child process completing, the parent kills the child with kill.

SUMMARY

Interrupts and exceptions are events that may occur when a program is running. Handler routines allow these signals to be trapped within the program.

The system call kill allows a process to send a signal to another process. The process sending the signal must send it to a child process or the process sending the signal must be owned by root.

EXERCISES

1. Write a program that displays all the processes you have running (by executing the command "ps ux" in system) and then continually prompts for process id numbers to kill. Specifying a process id of −1 exits the program. □

2. Modify a program you have previously written to prompt the user if he or she really wants to quit when cntl-c is typed. □

INTERPROCESS COMMUNICATION: SOCKETS

Unix is strongly based on the **client/server model**. A server process performs some service for a client. For example, whenever you telnet to a system, your telnet connection is handled by a telnet server. By typing telnet, the telnet process (client) requests the server to perform some service (telnet connection).

Many services such as line printing, telnet (login) connections, and electronic mail are handled by servers. A server process is also known as a daemon process. By convention, most server processes end with "d". For example, telnetd is the telnet server, ftpd is the FTP server, maild is the mail daemon, and lprd is the line printer daemon.

In the client/server model on Unix, there is initially only one server process for each service performed. A server process can only handle one client process at a time. Some server processes fork off a child process every time a client requests a service.

SOCKETS

The Berkeley version of Unix made a major change to the interprocess communication (IPC) of the AT&T version. Berkeley created the concept of sockets. **Sockets** are an attmept to make IPC look like file I/O.

175

They use the same read, write, and close system calls as file operations and use the file descriptor table.

Sockets are used for communication between unrelated processes (processes not created by forking a single original process). All the interprocess communication (IPC) between unrelated processes is done through sockets in Berkeley Unix.

DOMAINS

Berkeley IPC has two domains. Domains specify where two processes can communicate.

- The Unix domain is used for communication on the same machine. You cannot communicate between processes on two machines using Unix domain sockets.
- Internet domain sockets allow communication between two processes whether or not those processes exist on the same machine.

Unix domain sockets are useful for testing programs. Most people test out their programs using Unix domain sockets, and when convinced they work properly, change them to use Internet domain sockets.

SOCKET TYPES

A **socket type** defines the communication access method used to communicate between two sockets. There are three primary socket types in Berkeley Unix:

- **Stream sockets** use sequenced, reliable, bidirectional communication.
- **Datagram sockets** are bidirectional, but the communication is not guaranteed to be received in the same order it was sent.
- **Raw sockets** are for network programmers who want to define their own network protocol. (This topic is beyond the scope of this book.)

A stream socket is analogous to a telephone whereas a datagram is analogous to a post office box. Consider if you are in San Francisco and want to communicate with someone in Boston. One way to communicate is via the telephone. Once you have reached the person, every word you say is heard in order (sequential), every word you say will be heard on the other end (reliable), and the other person can talk back to you (bidirectional). Another way to communicate is via the post office. You can write down your message on several postcards and send them to Boston. It is not guaranteed that all your postcards will arrive in order (not sequenced), and the other person can communicate at the same time (bidirectional). Unlike the post office analogy, every datagram is guaranteed to arrive eventually.

INCLUDE FILE

Whenever you use sockets, the file /usr/include/sys/socket.h must be included in your program. This file defines the socket domain:

    AF_UNIX and AF_INET

and the socket type:

    SOCK_STREAM, SOCK_DGRAM, and SOCK_RAW

This file also contains the structure of the socket address:

```
struct sockaddr
  {
    u_short      sa_family; /* AF_INET or AF_UNIX */
    char         sa_data[14]; /* name of socket */
  } ;
```

EXAMPLE CLIENT/SERVER

Here are two examples of stream sockets. In the first example, a client (shown in Figure 17.1) will connect to a server (shown in Figure 17.2) and the client sends the message "hello". Remember that stream sockets are analogous to a telephone call.

This example is analogous to a telephone conversation where you call up a friend, say "hello," and hang up.

First of all, both of you must have a telephone to talk to each other. In Unix, both processes must create a socket to have a conversion. The format of the socket command is:

```
sd = socket(domain,socket_type,protocol)
   int sd          is a socket descriptor. Socket descriptors
                   work in the same manner as file descriptors.

   domain          is either AF_UNIX or AF_INET

   socket_type     is usually SOCK_STREAM or SOCK_DGRAM

   protocol        A protocol value of zero means to use the
                   default network protocol.
```

```
#include <sys/types.h>
#include <sys/socket.h>
#define SIZEOFSOCKNAME 10
/* 2 bytes (family) + 8 bytes for "greeting" (data) = 10 */
main()
  {
    int sd;
    struct  sockaddr sockname;

    sd = socket(AF_UNIX,SOCK_STREAM,0);
    sockname.sa_family = AF_UNIX;
    strcpy(sockname.sa_data,"greeting");

    if (connect(sd,&sockname,SIZEOFSOCKNAME) == -1)
      {
        perror("Bad connection");
        exit();
      }

    write(sd,"Hello",5);
    close(sd);
  }
```

FIGURE 17.1

In this example, both the client and the server have:

```
sd = socket(AF_UNIX,SOCK_STREAM,0);
```

SERVER

Your friend must have a telephone number registered with the telephone company so that when you dial your friend's telephone number, it knows to ring your friend's telephone.

In Unix, the server must register a name (telephone number) of a certain socket for any process to connect with it. The format of the bind command is:

```
bind(sd,soc_name,len_soc_name)          where
  int sd            is the socket descriptor
  soc_name          is the name to associate with the socket

  len_soc_name      is the length of your soc_name
```

The bind call will return an error code of -1 if the name could not be successfully registered.

```
#include <sys/types.h>
#include <sys/socket.h>
#define  SIZEOFSOCKNAME 10

main()
  {
    int    sd, ns;
    char   buf[256];
    struct sockaddr sockname;
    int    fromlen;
    int    i;

    sd = socket(AF_UNIX,SOCK_STREAM,0);
    sockname.sa_family = AF_UNIX;
    strcpy(sockname.sa_data,"greeting");

    if (bind(sd,&sockname,SIZEOFSOCKNAME) == -1)
      {
        perror("binding error");
        exit();
      }

    listen(sd,1);

    ns = accept(sd,&sockname,&fromlen);

    i = read(ns,buf,sizeof(buf));
    printf("Server received %s\n",buf);
    printf("It was %d bytes long\n",i);
    close(ns);
    close(sd);
    unlink(sockname.sa_data);
  }
```

FIGURE 17.2

In this example, the server code to register the name "greeting" for a socket is:

```
sa.sa_family = AF_UNIX;
strcpy(sa.sa_data,"greeting");
if (bind(sd,&sa,sizeof(sa)) == -1)
  { /* error condition */
    perror("Error in bind\n");
    close (sd);
    exit();
  }
```

sa is a variable containing the socket address. The value of sa is the position of the socket descriptor in the file descriptor table.

The next statement of the server is used to tell how many clients can be awaiting a connection at one time. The format of the listen call is:

```
listen (sd,awaiting_connections);
   int sd                     is the socket descriptor

       awaiting-connections  is the number of clients that
                             the server will allow to be
                             queued awaiting a connection.
```

If the queue is full, the client will be notified of the error.

A server waits until a client contacts it to have a service provided. The next statement causes the server to block until a client requests a service:

```
accept(sd, addr, addrlen);
   int sd       is the socket descriptor.

   addr     is address of the client connecting to the server.

   addrlen is the length of the server address.
```

Once a client connects to the server, the address of the client's socket is put in addr. If the server wants to, it can check the addr and refuse to communicate with certain clients. In almost all Unix servers, the value of addr and addrlen are ignored.

On return from the accept call, a new socket is created. This new socket is used for actually communicating with the client. The original socket is used to await more connections from other clients. The server may fork off a child process to handle the client connection on the new socket while the parent process awaits more clients on the original socket.

The following line of code from the server accepts a connection:

```
ns = accept(sd,&client_sa,&fromlen);
```

CLIENT

Now, let us take a look at the client.

The first thing the client does is to create a socket with the statement:

```
sd = socket(AF_UNIX,SOCK_STREAM,0)
```

The next thing that it does is to connect to the server's socket. In our telephone analogy, this is equivalent to dialing up your friend's telephone number. We must specify the name of the socket to which we wish to connect.

The format of the connect statement is:

```
connect(sd,soc_name,len_soc_name)     where
     int sd        is the socket descriptor.

     soc_name      is the name of the socket to connect to.

     len_soc_name is the length of soc_name.
```

In the example, the client performs the following code:

```
sa.sa_family = AF_UNIX;
strcpy(sa.sa_data,"greeting");
if (connect(sd,&sa,sizeof(sa)) == -1)
  {
    printf("Bad connection\n");
    close(sd);
    exit();
  }
```

If the client cannot connect to the server, the client will close its socket and exit. In watching students write Unix IPC programs, the four most common reasons for bad connections are:

1. The server is not running
2. An incorrect name or length of the name has been bound to the server socket
3. No name was bound to the server socket
4. More clients are awaiting a connection than specified in the servers' listen call

The next statement in the client is:

```
write(sd,"hello",6);
```

The last statement of the program:

```
close(sd);
```

will close the socket. One very important fact about the close statement is that when a socket is closed, it sends the EOF (end of file) character to the other socket. Unless a socket is closed, the other process does not know that communication has ended.

BACK TO THE SERVER

Back to the server process. We left off right after describing the accept statement. The next statement is:

```
read(ns,buf,sizeof(buf));
```

Again, this statement works exactly like the file I/O read statement. read will return the number of bytes read. The process will wait until either sizeof(buf) characters have been sent to the socket or EOF has been reached.

The last two statments of the server process close the two socket connections:

```
close(ns);
close(sd);
```

SEND AND RECV

With sockets, the system calls **send** and **recv** may be used instead of read and write to send information. The system call send works in the same manner as write, but it also allows information to be sent out of order. In addition to providing all the functionality of read, recv can peek at any received messages without actually reading them.

RUNNING THIS EXAMPLE

To run this example, first start the server process running in the background and then run the client process:

```
server1a &
client1a
```

The server must be run first because the name of the socket must be registered before the client connects with it. Both the client and the server must be run in the same directory because Unix domain socket bindings use the file system, and the socket named "greeting" appears in the directory where the server is running. To run the client and server in different directories, the absolute pathname must be specified (i.e., /tmp/greeting).

Figure 17.3 shows pictorially this process of the client and server communicating.

Server creates socket

Server binds name;
performs listen and accept

Client creates socket

Connect is performed

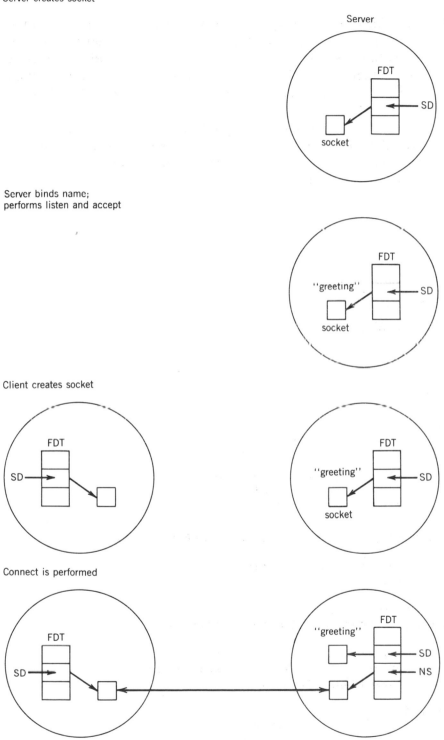

FIGURE 17.3

TWO-WAY COMMUNICATION

Sockets are bidirectional. Information can be sent in either direction—
even at the same time. This example also shows that even though the
server is sending a string of 38 bytes, the client can read it 5 bytes at
a time. The client sends "Hello" to the server and the server sends
back "World", and then it sends back "This line is more than 5 bytes
long".

The previous example had one major flaw in it—it did not follow the
true server model where the server continues to provide the service
to any other clients requesting the service. The addition of an infinite
for loop solves this problem.

Client

```
/* client2.c */
#include <sys/types.h>
#include <sys/socket.h>
#define SIZEOFSOCKNAME 4

main()
    {
        int       sd;
        int       i;
        char      buf[5];
        struct sockaddr sockname;

        sd = socket(AF_UNIX,SOCK_STREAM,0);
        sockname.sa_family = AF_UNIX;
        strcpy(sockname.sa_data,"sb");

        if (connect(sd,&sockname,SIZEOFSOCKNAME) == -1)
            {
                perror("Bad connection");
                exit();
            }
        write(sd,"Hello",5);
        while ((i = read(sd,buf,sizeof(buf))) > 0)
            {
                printf("Client received %s\n",buf);
                printf("It was %d bytes long\n \n",i);
                bzero(buf,sizeof(buf));
            }
        close(sd);
    }
```

Server

```
/* server2.c */
#include <sys/types.h>
#include <sys/socket.h>
#include <signal.h>
#define SIZEOFSOCKNAME 4

int sd;
struct sockaddr sockname;

int onintr()
    {
      close(sd);
      unlink(sockname.sa_data);
      exit();
    }


main()
    {
        int   ns;
        char buf[256];
        int   fromlen;

        sd = socket(AF_UNIX,SOCK_STREAM,0);
        sockname.sa_family - AF_UNIX;
        strcpy(sockname.sa_data,"sb");

        if (bind(sd,&sockname,SIZEOFSOCKNAME) == -1)
            {
                perror("binding error");
                exit();
            }

        listen(sd,1);

        signal(SIGINT,onintr);
        for(;;)
          {
            ns = accept(sd,&sockname,&fromlen);
            read(ns,buf,sizeof(buf)); /* ignore number of bytes */
            printf("Server received %s\n",buf);

            write(ns,"World",5);
            write(ns,"This line is more than five bytes long",38);
            close(ns);
          }

    }
```

RUNNING THE PROGRAM

First run server2a in the background and then run client2a:

```
server2a &
client2a
```

Make certain that you bring server2a back into the foreground with fg and type cntl-c. Otherwise, the socket binding is never removed.

FORKING A CHILD PROCESS

Some daemons must fork off child processes to handle connections because they must handle multiple connections at the same time. The telnet daemon is an example of this. It creates a child process for every telnet connection to the system.

The bookserver is an example of this kind of server. When it accepts a connection, the server forks off a child process to handle the connection. The parent process continues to wait around for more connections.

The client (bookauthor) reads the name of a book from standard input and sends this name to the server. The server returns the name of the author who wrote the book. When the client sends "Quit", the child process ends the connection and goes away.

Client

```
#include <sys/types.h>
#include <sys/socket.h>
#include <string.h>

main()
  {
    int     sd;
    struct  sockaddr sa;
    char    authorname[120];
    char    bookname[80];

    sd = socket(AF_UNIX,SOCK_STREAM,0);
    sa.sa_family = AF_UNIX;
    strcpy(sa.sa_data,"bookservice");
    if (connect(sd,&sa,sizeof(sa)) == -1)
      {
        perror("Bad connection in bookauthor");
        close(sd);
        exit();
      }
```

```
      scanf("%s",bookname);
      while ((strcmp(bookname,"Quit")) && (strcmp(bookname,"quit")))
        {
          write(sd,bookname,strlen(bookname));
          bzero(authorname,sizeof(authorname));
                        /* init buffer to binary zero */
          read(sd,authorname,sizeof(authorname));
          printf("%s\n\n",authorname);
          scanf("%s",bookname);
        }
      write(sd,"Quit",4);
      close(sd);
  }
```

Server

```
#include <sys/types.h>
#include <sys/socket.h>

int onintr()
  {
    close(sd);
    unlink(sockname.sa_data);
    exit();
  }

main()
  {
    int     sd, ns;
    char    buf[256];
    struct sockaddr sa, client_sa;
    int     fromlen;
    int     pid;

    sd = socket(AF_UNIX,SOCK_STREAM,0);
    sa.sa_family = AF_UNIX;
    strcpy(sa.sa_data,"bookservice");
    if (bind(sd,&sa,sizeof(sa)) == -1)
      {
        perror("Bad binding in bookserver");
        close(sd);
        exit();
      }

    signal(SIGINT,onintr);

    listen(sd,1);
```

```
for(;;)
  {
    ns = accept(sd,&client_sa,&fromlen);
    pid = fork()

    if (pid == -1)
      {
        perror("bad fork");
        exit();
      }

    if (pid == 0)
      {
        close(sd);
        bzero(buf,sizeof(buf));
        read(ns,buf,sizeof(buf));
        while (strcmp(buf,"Quit"))
          {
            if (! strcmp(buf,"Hobbit"))
              write(ns,"Tolkien",7);
            else if (! strcmp(buf,"Candide"))
              write(ns,"Voltaire",8);
            else if (! strcmp(buf,"1984"))
              write(ns,"Orwell",6);
            else if (! strcmp(buf,"Frankenstein"))
              write(ns,"Shelley",7);
            else
              write(ns,"Author Unknown",14);
            bzero(buf,sizeof(buf));
            read(ns,buf,sizeof(buf));
          }

        close(ns);
        exit();
      }
    else
      {
        close(ns);
      }
  }
}
```

To execute this program properly, the server (bookserver) must be run in the background and then the client (bookauthor) is run. When finished, the server needs to be brought back into the foreground and killed with cntl-c.

```
> bookserver &

> bookauthor
Candide
Voltaire
```

```
Hobbit
Tolkien

Quit

> bookauthor
1984
Orwell

Frankenstein
Shelley

Othello
Author Unknown

Quit

> fg
cntl-c
```

INTERNET SOCKETS

Internet sockets contain an internet address and port number. Each computer has a unique internet address. At one time, the file "/etc/hosts" contained a list of all names and addresses of hosts on the arpanet. With the new domain name software in Berkeley 4.3 BSD, each computer connects with a well-known computer at the site to find out the internet addresses of other computers. The file /etc/hosts contains at least the internet address of the computer being worked on and the address of the well-known host to find other internet addresses. This file contains the internet address and the name of the computer:

```
127.1            localhost
28.8.0.29        myhost
28.8.0.52        anotherhost
```

The file "/etc/services" contains a list of port numbers—one number for each daemon and the networking protocol used (TCP, PUP):

```
ftp         21/tcp
telnet      23/tcp
finger      79/tcp
```

Two additional include files are needed when using internet sockets:

- /usr/include/netinet/in.h
- /usr/include/netdb.h

The important data types from these include files are:

```
/* format of name to bind or connect to a socket */
struct sockaddr_in {
  short       sin_family;        /** usually host address type **/
  u_short     sin_port;          /** port number **/
  struct      in_addr sin_addr;  /** address of host **/
  char        sin_zero[8];
};

/* structure of information from /etc/hosts */
struct hostent {
  char        *h_name;           /* official name of host */
  char        **h_aliases;       /* alias list */
  int         h_addrtype;        /* host address type */
  int         h_length;          /* length of address */
  char        **h_addr_list;     /* list of addresses */
};

/* structure of information from /etc/services */
struct servent {
  char        *s_name;           /* official service name */
  char        **s_aliases;       /* alias list */
  int         s_port;            /* port # */
  char        *s_proto;          /* protocol to use */
};

/** these functions return host and IP socket information **/
struct hostent  *gethostbyname(), *gethostbyaddr(),
*gethostent();
struct netent   *getnetbyname(), *getnetbyaddr(), *getnetent();
struct servent  *getservbyname(), *getservbyport(),
*getservent();
struct protoent *getprotobyname(), *getprotobynumber(),
*getprotoent();
```

This first example shows two-way interprocess communication. The server sends "hello" to the client and the client sends "world" to the server. Use a port number not listed in the /etc/services file. For these programs, the number 787 has been arbitrarily chosen.

The proper method for a well-known server is to register a port number with the system manager and have it listed in the /etc/services file. The port number is then found by:

```
struct servent *sp;

sp = getservbyname("service","tcp");
if (sp == NULL)
  {
    fprintf(stderr,"unknown service error");
    exit();
  }
```

where "service " is the name of the service provided by the server. The string "tcp " should be used if the client and server use TCP-IP to communicate.

The only difference between Unix domain and internet domain sockets is the way they are created:

```
sd = socket(AF_UNIX,SOCK_STREAM,0);

sd = socket(AF_INET,SOCK_STREAM,0);
```

and the way names are bound to the socket:

```
sa.sa_family = AF_UNIX;
strcpy(sa.sa_data,"bookservice");
if (connect(sd,&sa,sizeof(sa)) == -1)

hp = gethostbyname("MyHost");
bzero((char *)&sin,sizeof(sin));
bcopy(hp->h_addr,(char *)&sin.sin_addr,hp->h_length);
sin.sin_port - MYPORT;
sin.sin_family = h->h_addrtype;
if (connect(sd,(char *)&sin,sizeof(sin)) == -1)
```

INTERNET EXAMPLE

This example is the internet version of an example shown previously in this chapter (under two-way communication). The client sends "Hello" to the server, and the server sends back "World".

```
Client

#include <sys/types.h>
#include <sys/socket.h>
#include <netdb.h>
#include <netinet/in.h>
#define MYPORT  787

main()
  {
    int     sd;
    char    buf[256];
    struct  servent         *sp;
    struct  hostent         *hp;
    struct  sockaddr_in     sin;

    sd = socket(AF_INET,SOCK_STREAM,0);

    /* get the host information including IP address */
    hp = gethostbyname("MyHost");
```

```
      bzero((char *)&sin,sizeof(sin));

      /* Copy the IP address in hp to sin */
      bcopy(hp->h_addr,(char *)&sin.sin_addr,hp->h_length);

      /* assign port ID */
      sin.sin_port = MYPORT;

      /* specift address type */
      sin.sin_family = hp->h_addrtype;

      /* note sin variable used in connect */
      if (connect(sd,(char *)&sin,sizeof(sin)) == -1)
        {
          perror("Bad connection");
          exit();
        }

    read(sd,buf,sizeof(buf));
    printf("Client receives %s\n",buf);
    write(sd,"World",5);
    close(sd);
  }
```

The server must have the same port number defined for MYPORT
as the server1.c program.

```
    #include <sys/types.h>
    #include <sys/socket.h>
    #include <netdb.h>
    #include <netinet/in.h>
    #define MYPORT  787
    main()
      {
        int sd, ns;
        char buf[256];
        struct sockaddr sockaddr;
        int fromlen;

        struct    servent      *sp;
        struct    hostent      *hp;
        struct    sockaddr_in  sin;

        sd = socket(AF_INET,SOCK_STREAM,0);

        /* port information */
        hp     = gethostbyname("MyHost");
        bzero((char *)&sin,sizeof(sin));
        bcopy(hp->h_addr,(char *)&sin.sin_addr,hp->h_length);
        sin.sin_port      = MYPORT;
        sin.sin_family    = hp->h_addrtype;
```

```
if (bind(sd,(char *)&sin,sizeof(sin)) == -1)
  {
    perror("error in bind");
    exit();
  }

listen(sd,1);

for(;;)
  {
    ns = accept(sd,&sockaddr,&fromlen);
    write(ns,"Hello",5);
    read(ns,buf,sizeof(buf));
    printf(" %s\n",buf);
    close(ns);
  }
}
```

DATAGRAM SOCKETS

The idea behind datagram sockets is that the server does not bind and the client does not connect. Instead, the bind or connect information is sent out along with the data information.

So far, only stream sockets have been used in this chapter. The programs client3.c and server3.c use datagram sockets. Recall that communication with datagrams is analogous to sending postcards via the post office.

The sendto system call in client3.c is equivalent to a connect, and then a write. The recvfrom system call is equivalent to an accept, and then a read.

The server is located on a system called **hostb**. The client may be used from any system including hostb.

Unlike the previous example, this server does not assume that it is working on a certain host. Instead of having the hostname as a constant in the program, the system call gethostname is used to get the hostname when the server is running.

Client

```
#include <sys/types.h>
#include <sys/socket.h>
#include <netdb.h>
#include <netinet/in.h>
#define MYPORT  787 /* this port number must not */
                    /* be used in /etc/services  */
```

```
main()
  {
    int     sd;
    char    buf[256];

    struct    servent         *sp;
    struct    hostent         *hp;
    struct    sockaddr_in     sin;

    sd = socket(AF_INET,SOCK_DGRAM,0);   /* note datagram type */

    hp     = gethostbyname("hostb");
    bzero((char *)&sin,sizeof(sin));
    bcopy(hp->h_addr,(char *)&sin.sin_addr,hp->h_length);
    sin.sin_port      = MYPORT;
    sin.sin_family    = hp->h_addrtype;

    /* notice no connect is needed */
    sendto(sd,"hello",5,0,(char *)&sin,sizeof(sin));
  }


Server

#include <sys/types.h>
#include <sys/socket.h>
#include <netdb.h>
#include <netinet/in.h>
#define MYPORT  787

main()
  {
    int     sd, ns;
    char    buf[256];
    struct  sockaddr sockaddr;
    int     fromlen;
    char    myname[32];

    struct  servent         *sp;
    struct  hostent         *hp;
    struct  sockaddr_in     sin;

    sd = socket(AF_INET,SOCK_DGRAM,0);

    /* proper way to access gethostbyname. */
        /* Does not assume "hostb" */
    if (gethostname(myname, sizeof(myname) - 1) < 0)
      {
        perror("gethostname problem");
        exit();
      }

    printf("hostname : %s\n",myname);
    hp     = gethostbyname(myname);
```

```
    bzero((char *)&sin,sizeof(sin));
    bcopy(hp->h_addr,(char *)&sin.sin_addr,hp->h_length);
    sin.sin_port    = MYPORT;
    sin.sin_family  = hp->h_addrtype;

    if (bind(sd,(char *)&sin,sizeof(sin)) == -1)
        {
          perror("Error in bind");
          exit();
        }

    for(;;)
        {
          recvfrom(sd,buf,sizeof(buf),0,&sockaddr,&fromlen);
          printf("Server received %s\n",buf);
        }
}
```

SUMMARY

Sockets were created to make interprocess communication look like file I/O. Unix is strongly based on the client/server model. The server provides some service, and the client connects to the server to get this service. Interprocess communication is either in the Unix domain or the Internet domain. Internet domain communication between a client and a server can either be on the same machine or between two different machines. Unix domain communication must be between a client and a server on the same machine. The client and server communicate with stream sockets or datagram sockets.

The server often forks off a child process to handle communication with the client process. The parent process continues to wait for clients to request a service.

EXERCISES

1. Modify the bookserver to read the list of books and authors from a file called bookdata instead of having this list coded in the program. ☐

2. Remote command execution. Create a client/server pair. The client continually sends the name of a command to the server, the server executes the command, and sends the output back to the client.

The client displays this output. When the client sends "`quit`", the communication with the server should be terminated. Use internet domain sockets for this assignment. Your solution must be able to run the server on a different host from the client and run multiple clients at the same time. ☐

CHAPTER 18

SCREEN MANIPULATION: CURSES

Unix is used on a wide variety of computer architectures. More than 500 terminal and workstation devices are defined in the /etc/termcap file. This file defines the characteristics of your terminal type. For example, if your terminal type is defined to be a vt100 terminal, the system knows the terminal definition because of the entries in /etc/termcap.

Imagine trying to write a software package requiring screen manipulation for 500 different terminal types—each one with its own defined character set. The curses package provides a mechanism for manipulating screen information. All the curses routines rely on the terminal definition being specified correctly with "setenv TERM". Curses looks at the TERM variable and then searches for the terminal definition in the /etc/termcap file. The information in /etc/termcap describes the special characters needed for the terminal screen. You do not have to worry about using the information in /etc/termcap, because the curses terminal package takes care of this.

The curses package uses the following coordinates for the x and y axis of your terminal (assuming a 24 by 80 character terminal):

```
                            Y

                1           2           7

       01234567890          0    ....    9


                ----------------------    ------

          0 |                              |

          1 |                              |

     X    2 |                              |

          . |                              |

          . |                              |

          . |                              |

         23 |  ----------------------      |
             ----------------------    ------
```

Editors such as emacs and vi make extensive use of screen manipulation. In this chapter, the curses package is explained by creating an emacs program.

FIRST EXAMPLE : EMACS1

This simple example (Fig. 18.1) shows the very basic of the curses package. It shows how to use the following curses routines:

- `initscr()` : Create a window
- `endwin()` : End a window
- `move(x,y)` : Move the curser to an *x-y* coordinate
- `getch()` : Get a character
- `noecho()` : Do not echo characters as soon as they are typed
- `raw()` : No characters (including cntl-c) have any special meaning
- `insch(character)` : Insert a character on the screen
- `refresh()` : Display changes on the terminal

This version of emacs handles cntl-f, cntl-b, cntl-n, cntl-p, cntl-m (return key), and exits when cntl-c is typed. It will not save the contents of what is typed.

In this program, a window is created, raw mode is selected so that control characters are handled in the program, and characters are not echoed when they are typed. The characters are not echoed because

```c
#include <signal.h>
#include <curses.h>
#include <stdio.h>

main()
{
  int row,col;
  char c;

  row = 0;
  col = 0;

  initscr();
  raw();
  noecho();

  while(1)    /* infinite loop until cntl-c */
    {
      if (row < 0) row = 0;
      if (row > 23) row = 23;
      if (col < 0) col = 0;
      if (col > 79) col = 79;
      move(row,col);
      refresh();
      c = getch();

      if (c == '\006')   /* cntl-f */
        col++;
      else if (c == '\002')   /* cntl-b */
        col--;
      else if (c == '\016')   /* cntl-n */
        row++;
      else if (c == '\020')   /* cntl-p */
        row--;
      else if (c == '\015')   /* cntl-m - return key */
        {
          row++;
          col = 0;
        }
      else if (c == '\003')   /* cntl-c */
        {
          move(LINES-1, 0);
          refresh();
          endwin();
          exit();
        }
      else
        {
          insch(c);
          col++;
        }
    }
}
```

FIGURE 18.1

the program inserts them on the screen in the proper location using insch.

A loop is performed until cntl-c is typed. Move to the proper location on the screen, refresh the screen to display any changes, get the character, and perform the operation. For control characters except cntl-c, the operation performed is to change the row or column position. A cntl-c will end the window and exit the program. A character that is not one of the defined control characters is displayed on the screen. The variables row and col have the current row and column position.

COMPILING PROGRAMS WITH CURSES

A program using curses must be linked with the curses and termcap library routines when the executable is being created. To compile this emacs1 program properly, use:

```
cc -c emacs1.c
cc emacs1.o -o emacs1 -lcurses -ltermcap
```

ADDITIONAL FEATURES : EMACS2

This second version of the program (Fig. 18.2) adds several features to emacs. First, it is a true editor—the characters that are typed are stored in a buffer and a cntl-s will save the contents of the first 21 rows of the buffer to a file. When doing a cntl-s, the user is prompted for the filename. When prompting for the filename, the program must go to noraw mode to get the string. A signal is used to trap cntl-c's when the user is typing in the filename. This signal is necessary—otherwise, it is possible for the program to exit without executing endwin. Note that a cntl-c in the program now exists by also calling this handler routine from the program.

A cntl-o will insert a line and a cntl-k will delete a line—using the curses routines insertln and deleteln. Most of the code in the insertline and deleteline procedures of this program will move lines in the buffer to correspond to what is shown on the screen.

The savefile procedure prompts for a file to save the contents of the buffer. The initialization procedure initializes the row, col, cntl-c interrupt handler, and all the necessary curses initialization routines.

This program uses the routine addch instead of insch. This causes characters to be overwritten instead of being inserted as was done for the first program. Emacs normally inserts text instead of overwriting it, but it is easier to just overwrite text when working with the buffers— otherwise you must move the characters in a line of text every time a character is typed.

This program will also ignore control characters, which are not defined. Some additional curses features used are:

- `insertln()` : Insert a line
- `deleteln()` : Delete a line
- `standout()` : Print text in reverse video
- `standend()` : End reverse video
- `addch(c)` : Like insch, but overwritten instead of inserted
- `addstr(string)` : Like addch for an entire string
- `getstr(string)` : Like getch for an entire string
- `noraw()` : Get out of raw mode
- `echo()` : Echo characters

```
#include <signal.h>
#include <curses.h>
#include <stdio.h>

int row,col;
char buffer[21][80];   /* assuming 24 by 80 terminal */
                       /* first 21 rows are for text */
endpgm()
  {
    move(LINES-1, 0);  /* value of LINES set by curses package */
    refresh();
    endwin();
    exit();
  }
deleteline()
{
  int x,y;

  deleteln();               /* delete line on screen */

  for (x=row;x<19;x++)    /* delete line in buffer */
    for(y=0;y<79;y++)
      buffer[x][y] = buffer[x+1][y];
```

```
  for(y=0;y<79;y++)      /* initialize last line in buffer */
    buffer[20][y] = ' ';

  col = 0;
}

insertline()
{
  int x,y;

  insertln();            /* insert line on screen */

  for (x=19;x>=row;x--)  /* insert line in buffer */
    for(y=0;y<79;y++)
      buffer[x+1][y] = buffer[x][y];

  for(y=0;y<79;y++)      /* initialize line */
    buffer[row][y] = ' ';

  col = 0;
}
/* save the contents of the buffer to a filename */
savefile()
{
  int x;
  FILE *fd;
  char thefilename[50];

  /* prompt for the name of the file */
  move(22,20);
  addstr("File:");
  refresh();

  /* get name of the file */

  noraw();               /* Impossible to get a string while in */
  echo();                /* raw mode. Note that cntl-c is trapped */
  getstr(thefilename);   /* by signal when not in raw mode. */
  raw();
  noecho();

  /* print out the file */
  fd = fopen (thefilename,"w");
  if (fd != NULL)
    {
      for (x=0; x<21; x++)
        {
          fprintf(fd,"%s\n",buffer[x]);
        }
      fclose(fd);
      move(22,20);
      addstr("                                              ");
      refresh();
    }
```

```
    else
      {
        move(22,20);
        addstr("File could not be written              ");
        refresh();
      }
}

initialize()
{
  for(row=0;row<21;row++)
    for(col=0;col<79;col++)
      buffer[row][col] = ' ';

  row = 0;
  col = 0;

  signal(SIGINT, endpgm);

  initscr();
  raw();
  noecho();

  move(23,20);
  /* print in reverse mode */
  standout();
  addstr("myemacs - My version of Emacs");
  standend();

}
main()
{
  char c;

  initialize();

  while(1)   /* infinite loop until cntl-c */
    {
      if (row < 0) row = 0;
      if (row > 21) row = 21;
      if (col < 0) col = 0;
      if (col > 79) col = 79;

      move(row,col);
      refresh();
      c = getch();

      if (c == '\006')  /* cntl-f */
        col++;
      else if (c == '\002')  /* cntl-b */
        col--;
      else if (c == '\016')  /* cntl-n */
        row++;
```

```
    else if (c == '\020')  /* cntl-p */
      row--;
    else if (c == '\015')  /* cntl-m */
      {
        row++;
        col = 0;
      }
    else if (c == '\001')  /* cntl-a */
      col = 0;
    else if (c == '\013')  /* cntl-k */
      deleteline();
    else if (c == '\017')  /* cntl-o */
      insertline();
    else if (c == '\023')  /* cntl-s */
      savefile();
    else if (c == '\003')  /* cntl-c */
      endpgm();
    else if (c > '\032')    /* if c > cntl-z */
      /* ignore control characters not defined */
      {
        addch(c);
        buffer[row][col] = c;
        col++;
      }
    }
  }
}
```

FIGURE 18.2

OTHER IMPORTANT CURSES ROUTINES

The curses package has many screen manipulation routines. Only the most important can be mentioned in this book. For a complete list, look in the online manual pages under curses. Two important routines worth mentioning that were not used are:

```
clear() /* clears the screen */
```

and

```
getxy (stdscr, row, col)
     stdscr - defined by curses (standard screen)
     int row, col
```

getxy is a macro that gets the *x-y* position of the cursor.

EXERCISES

1. Modify the emacs2 program to insert characters on the screen instead of overwriting characters.   □

2. Modify emacs2 to have a buffer size of 100 and allow pages of text to be scrolled on the screen. Implement the control sequence cntl-v to move down a screenful of text.   □

## PART FOUR

MISCELLANEOUS UNIT TOPICS

CHAPTER 19

DOCUMENT PREPARATION

DOCUMENT PROCESSING PACKAGES

All Unix systems come with the nroff/troff document processing package. Some systems may also have the TeX/LaTex or the Scribe document preparation system; check with your local system administrator for more information. This chapter describes the nroff/troff package because it is available on all Unix systems and is used to create online help pages for the man command.

The **troff** command takes a document and produces output that can be printed on laser printers and displayed on graphic terminals. The **nroff** command takes the same document and produces output for viewing on CRT terminals and daisy-wheel printers. Document formatting in nroff/troff is performed by using functions, primitive requests, and macros.

FUNCTIONS

All functions begin with a "\" escape character. To print a "\" in the document, a "\e" must be used. The name of the function follows the escape character. Functions are most often used to switch between different font types:

  \fR   Roman font
  \fI   Italic font (reverse video on CRT terminals)
  \fB   Bold font (standard roman text on CRT devices)
  \fP   Revert back to the previous font

For example, a document containing:

```
cp [\fB-i\fR] [\fB-r\fR] \fIfile1 file2\fR
```

is formatted as:

```
cp [-i] [-r] file1 file2
```

PRIMITIVE REQUESTS AND MACROS

Both primitive requests and macros begin with a period and must start on a new line. Primitive requests have lowercase letters; macros have uppercase letters. Macros and primitive requests may have zero, one, or several arguments, depending on their use. For example, the primitive request sp inserts a certain number of blank lines:

```
.sp n
```

where n is the number of blank lines to insert. If n is not specified, a single blank line is inserted.

FONTS

The font type may be changed with macros as well as functions. The following macros are used to change fonts:

  .B [word(s)]   Bold
  .I [word(s)]   Italicize
  .R   Return to roman font
  .UL   Underline words

If one or more words are arguments to the macro, the words will be displayed in that specified font type. If no words are arguments to the macro, then all the text on the following line is displayed in that font type. For example, arguments are specified after the bold macro, but italicize has no arguments. The following example shows Figure 19.1 using these font macros:

```
The mode and owner of
.B file2
are preserved if it already
existed;
.I
the mode of the source file
is used otherwise
```

FIGURE 19.1

The mode and owner of file2 are preserved if it already existed; the mode of the source file is used otherwise.

PARAGRAPHS

A paragraph macro must preceed every new paragraph.

.PP   Paragraph (first line indented)
.LP   Left-aligned paragraph
.IP   Indented paragraph
.XP   Paragraph (all but first line indented)

HEADING AND TITLE MACROS

These macros are used to print page headings and titles in documents:

.TH   Display title heading on every page
.SH   Section heading
.NH   Numbered heading

ALIGNMENT FORMATS

These alignment formats specify the alignment of text in the document. The TP macro:

```
.TP [position]
```

sets up a tabbed environment. If a position is specified, this is the number of characters to tab over; if position is omitted, the distance to tab over is the same as the last use of TP. The first line after the TP macro starts at the lefthand margin of the page. Following lines will start in the column given by position.

The IP macro creates an indented paragraph with a label in the left margin:

```
.IP label position
```

The position is the position to tab over.

The ti request is used to tab the next line over a certain distance:

```
.ti position
```

POSITION VALUES

A variety of units may be specified for the position parameters:

- c: Centimeters
- i: Inches
- m: Ems (width of the letter m)
- n: Ens (width of the letter n)
- p: Points (1/72nd of an inch)

The position value is given, followed by the unit:

- 3.1c: 3.1 centimeters
- 1.5i: 1.5 inches
- 144p: 144 points (2 inches)

If the unit is not specified, the default unit depends on the macro or primitive request.

RIGHT MARGINS

Different right margin formats can be set:

- `.ad`: Adjusted right formats
- `.na`: Do not adjust lines
- `.nf`: Copy lines verbatim to the output

By default, troff/nroff adjust the text to line up the right margin.

WRITING MANUAL PAGES

Every command should have a manual page describing its usage. All the manual pages are located in the directory /usr/man. Manual pages are placed in the appropriate subdirectory depending on the section of the manual where they belong. The nroff documents for manual pages in section 1 are placed in man1; section 2 pages are placed in man2; and so on. The suffix of the filename also specifies the correct section number. For example, the cp command is in section 1 of the manual. The filename for the manual page is cp.1, and it is located in /usr/man/man1/cp.1.

From the nroff documents, files are processed that can be displayed on the screen. All these files are located in a corresponding cat subdirectory depending on the section number: /usr/man/cat1, /usr1/man/cat2, and so on. To format a manual page for the cp command, use:

```
nroff -man /usr/man/man1/cp.1 > /usr/man/cat1/cp.1
```

Note that the -man option must be specified to nroff when processing an online manual document to create the proper format. If someone executes the statement man cp and the /usr/man/man1/cp.1 files exits while the /usr/man/cat1/cp.1 does not exist, the /usr/man/cat1/cp.1 file will be automatically created.

A DETAILED MANUAL EXAMPLE

This section shows the nroff document and the output of a manual page for the cp command. All the functions, primitive requests, and macros used in this document were previously described in this chapter. All the manual pages follow this same basic format. A ".\" at the beginning of a line is a line comment. A "\"" causes the rest of the line to be a comment.

Figure 19.2 shows the /usr/man/man1/cp.1 document file.

```
.\ Manual page for the cp command
.TH cp 1                                    \" title heading
.SH NAME                                    \" sub heading
cp - copy file data
.SH SYNTAX
.B cp                                       \" bold primitive request
[\fB-i\fR] [\fB-r\fR] \fIfile1 file2\fR     \" func. for font change
.PP
.B cp
[\fB-i\fR] [\fB-r\fR] \fIfile... directory\fR
.SH DESCRIPTION
The cp command copies
.I File1
onto
.IR file2 .
The mode and owner of
.I file2
are preserved if it already
existed; the mode of the source file
is used otherwise.
.PP                                         \" new paragraph
In the second form, one or more
.I files
are copied into the
.I directory
with their original file-names.
.PP
The cp command refuses to copy a file onto itself.
.SH OPTIONS
.TP 20\" Set tab position at 20 characters. Next line (-i) starts
.B\-i\" at left margin. Following lines to next TP start in col 20
Prompts user with the name of file
whenever the copy will cause an old file to be
overwritten. An answer of 'y' will cause cp
to continue. Any other answer will prevent it
from overwriting the file.
.TP
.B\-r
Copies only to directories
.SH "SEE ALSO"
cat(1), pr(1), mv(1)
```

FIGURE 19.2

UNIX PROGRAMMER'S MANUAL

NAME

    cp - copy file data

SYNTAX

    cp [-i] [-r] file1 file2

    cp [-i] [-r] file ... directory

DESCRIPTION

The cp command copies file1 onto file2. The mode and owner of file2 are preserved if it already existed; the mode of the source file is used otherwise.

In the second form, one or more files are copied into the directory with their original filenames.

The cp command refuses to copy a file onto itself.

OPTIONS

-i Prompts the user with the name of the file whenever the copy will cause an old file to be overwritten. An answer of 'y' will cause cp to continue. Any other answer will prevent it from overwriting the file.

-r Copies only to directories.

SEE ALSO

    cat(1), pr(1), mv(1)

FIGURE 19.3. Output of Figure 19.2.

Figure 19.3 presents the output of Figure 19.2.

Some manual pages use the IP macro instead of TP. The ls manual page is an example of this. Figure 19.4 shows a section of the ls manual page.

```
.IP \fB-a\fR 20
Displays all entries including those beginning with a period (.).
.IP \fB\-C\fR 20
Forces multicolumn output for pipe or filter. This is the default
when the output is to a terminal.
.IP \fB\-c\fR 20
Sorts entries by time of modification. Default is by name.
.IP \fB\-d\fR 20
Displays names of directories only, not contents.
Use this option
with \fB\-l\fR to get the status of
a directory.
.IP \fB\-F\fR 20
Marks directories with trailing slash (/), sockets
with a trailing equal sign (=), symbolic links with a trailing
at sign (@),
and executable files with a trailing asterisk (*).
```

FIGURE 19.4

This produces Figure 19.5 as its output.

-a	Displays all entries including those beginning with a period (.).
-C	Forces multicolumn output for pipe or filter. This is the default when the output is to a terminal.
-c	Sorts entries by time of modification. Default is by name.
-d	Displays names of directories only, not contents. Use this option with -l to get the status of a directory.
-F	Marks directories with trailing slash (/), sockets with a trailing equal sign (=), symbolic links with a trailing at sign (@), and executable files with a trailing asterisk (*).

FIGURE 19.5. Output of Figure 19.4.

FORMATTING LETTERS

Figure 19.6 shows the syntax to format a letter (letter is in a file called troffletter) and Figure 19.7 shows a sample letter created by troff/nroff using the syntax. The in request is used to reset the left margin. The nf macro must be used so that the name and address are not merged together on the same line. The nf formatting is turned off by the na request.

Letters and reports must use the ms macro package. This package is used by including the -ms option with the troff and nroff commands.

```
nroff -ms troffletter

or

troff -ms troffletter


.in 4i
.nf
James Wilson
2188 Ralmar Ave.
East Palo Alto CA 94303
.in   .1i
.sp 5

To: Speedy Electronics
    111 University Ave.
    Palo Alto CA 94301
.na
.sp3
.PP
Thank you for sending the necessary parts.
I appreciate your excellent and expedient service...
.sp 2
.PP
Enclosed is a check for the necessary amount.
.in 4i
.sp 2
Sincerely,
.sp 2
James Wilson
```

FIGURE 19.6

```
                                James Wilson
                                2188 Ralmar Ave.
                                East Palo Alto CA 94303

To: Speedy Electronics
    111 University Ave.
    Palo Alto CA 94301

Thank you for sending the necessary parts.  I appreciate your
excellent and expedient service...

Enclosed is a check for the necessary amount.

                                Sincerely,

                                James Wilson
```

FIGURE 19.7. Output of Figure 19.6.

FORMATTING REPORTS

Several additional macros needed to format reports are:

- .AB .AE: Start and end of abstract paragraph
- .AI: Author's institution
- .AU: Name of the author
- .FS .FE: Start and end of footnote
- .TL: Title heading

Figure 19.8 shows the format of a report file called troffreport. Figure 19.9 shows the output.

```
nroff -ms troffreport

or

troff -ms troffreport


.TL \" Title
An Analysis of the Literary Works of H.G. Wells
.AU \" Author Name
Dr. Ima Pseudonym
.AI \" Author Institute
Institute of Science Fiction Writing
.sp 2
.AB \" Start of abstract
A variety of novels and short stories are analyzed.
.AE \" End of abstract
.NH
Introduction
.PP
Body of introduction.
.NH
Novels
.NH 2
War of the Worlds
.PP
Discussion of "War of the Worlds."
.NH 2
Food of the Gods
.PP
Discussion of "Food of the Gods."
.NH
Short Stories
.PP
Body of short stories paragraph.
.sp 3
References
.sp
.IP 1.
first reference
.IP 2.
second reference
```

FIGURE 19.8

An Analysis of the Literary Works of H.G. Wells

Dr. Ima Pseudonym

Institute of Science Fiction Writing

ABSTRACT

A variety of novels and short stories are analyzed.

1. Introduction

Body of introduction.

2. Novels

2.1. War of the Worlds

Discussion of "War of the Worlds."

2.2. Food of the Gods

Discussion of "Food of the Gods."

3. Short Stories

Body of short stories paragraph.

References

1.   first reference

2.   second reference

FIGURE 19.9. Output of Figure 19.8.

SUMMARY

This chapter described how to create manual pages and simple letters and reports. For additional information on nroff/troff, your Unix system should come with complete written documentation on using the nroff/troff package. This documentation describes all the functions, primitive requests, and macros.

EXERCISES

For both these exercises, use nroff/troff:

1. Create a manual page describing some program or shell program that you have implemented. □

2. Create a letter or report of your choice. □

CHAPTER 20

SYSTEM MANAGEMENT

One disadvantage of a Unix computer system over a personal computer is that a Unix computer requires some system management. However, the basic management of a Unix system can be easily performed. Some of these system-management functions are:

1. Adding new users
2. Performing tape backups
3. Setting up servers
4. Making hardware devices
5. Restarting the print queue
6. Creating mailing aliases

ADDING NEW USERS

Different Unix systems have different means of adding users to the system. Refer to the system documentation to find the proper program to do this. Some systems have a program /etc/nu to add and delete users. This program prompts for information such as name, password, groups, default shell, and location of the home directory. When an account is created, nu creates a directory for the user, copies the default hidden files in /usr/skel to the user's home directory, and sets file ownership and permission information of the user's hidden files.

If nu or some similar program is not available, the program vipw edits the /etc/passwd file using the vi editor. Before running vipw, you must create the user directory and copy in the appropriate files. After running vipw, you must set the file permissions correctly.

The /etc/passwd file contains the following fields separated by colons:

1. Account name
2. Encrypted password
3. Primary group
4. User id
5. Name of person
6. Home directory
7. Default shell

For example:

```
me:sEe97b4rgA1hw:10:20:My Account:/usr/users/me:/bin/csh
```

Each account must have a unique user id. If two accounts have the same id, the two accounts are the same and may access each other's files.

Adding a User to Another Group

Each user has a default group to which it belongs. The /etc/passwd file contains the group id number of the user's primary group. To add the user to another group, edit the /etc/group file—adding the user's name to the list of people in the group.

The file /etc/group contains a list of valid groups. This file contains the following information:

1. Group name
2. Password—a "*" means no password is needed
3. Group id number
4. List of users in this group (but not primary)

The /etc/group file looks like the following:

```
staff:*:8:root,me,jw
```

Shutting Down and Rebooting the System

The command /etc/shutdown shuts down a system. This shutdown can bring the system to single-user mode or shut it down completely.

The command /etc/reboot reboots a machine from single-user mode to multiple-user mode. The command halt shuts down a machine completely from a single-user mode. The format of /etc/shutdown is:

```
/etc/shutdown options time message
```

The options are:

- -r : Shut down the system to single-user mode, and then reboot to multiple-user mode
- -h : Halt the system completely

Unless one of these options is specified, the system will be brought down to single-user mode.

The time is in one of three formats:

1. now : Specifying now as the shutdown time brings the system down immediately
2. +number : Brings the system down in a certain number of minutes
3. hour:min : Brings the system down at the given hour and minute

Users are notified at hourly intervals that the system is going down. They are also notified of shutdown 5 minutes before it occurs. The message is displayed on all terminals at the same time the shutdown message appears.

Reboot and Halt

In single-user mode, /etc/reboot brings the system to multiple-user mode. In single-user mode, typing halt will halt the system. Before typing halt , you should type sync a couple of times to sync the disks before halting.

When bringing a system from single-user to multiple-user mode, it looks at the files /etc/rc and /etc/rc.local for the actions to perform. To modify the sequence of booting events, edit the file /etc/rc.local.

The servers are created when a Bourne shell program called /etc/rc.local is executed. To stop running a server (such as ftpd, lpd, telnetd), comment out the appropriate lines of /etc/rc.local. Do not delete lines in these files in case someone wants these servers turned on at a later time. When adding a server to /etc/rc.local, follow the format of the other servers.

PERFORMING TAPE BACKUPS

The /etc/dump and /etc/restore commands dump and restore files from an entire partition.

The program /etc/dump has several advantages over the tar command. First, the /etc/fstab file tells how often the partition should be dumped. If the partition is not dumped within this number of days, the computer sends electronic mail to the system managers. Second, data are more compact, so more files fit on a tape under /etc/dump than tar. Third, dump can also handle situations where more information needs to be saved than can fit on a tape. Fourth, dump has different levels to minimize the amount of time spent waiting for a partition to be saved to tape.

The format of /etc/dump is:

```
/etc/dump level partition
```

The partition may be the actual device name (/dev/hd0b) or the partition name (/usr). Some options are available for this command—see the online manual for more information.

Although /etc/dump works when the system is in multiuser mode, there is a chance of losing a few files because of changing file inode numbers. For this reason, the system should be in single-user mode before a dump is performed.

Dump levels tell which files to dump based on their last modification date. A level-zero dump dumps every file in the partition to tape. Other dump levels dump all files modified or added since the last dump at a lower level. The following schedule of dump levels is designed to minimize the amount of time dumping files to tape and the amount of time required to restore files. Level-nine backups are performed nightly while the system is running in multiuser mode. Weekly backups are performed while the system is in single-user mode.

Week	Level
1	0
2	3
3	2
4	5
5	4
6	1
7	8
8	6
9	7

Another algorithm suggested in the online manual for systems that must be dumped nightly is:

Day	Level
1	3
2	2
3	5
4	4
5	7
6	6
7	9
8	8
9	9
10	9

RESTORING FILES

Unless you need to restore all the files in a partition, the best way to restore files is using the interactive option of /etc/restore. This mode allows you to go through dumped files using a subset of the file commands (ls, pwd, cd). The add command marks a file to restore. Delete unmarks a file. The extract command restores all the marked files.

To use restore in interactive mode, type:

```
/etc/restore i
```

To restore all the files, type:

```
/etc/restore
```

This program prompts you to start mounting all the necessary tapes—beginning with the level-zero dump and going up to the most recent level. This command prompts for the dump level you are restoring.

RESTARTING THE PRINT QUEUE

The /etc/lpc program controls the operation of the line printers. The format of this program is:

```
/etc/lpc/command
```

Some possible commands are:

- `help` : List available commands
- `abort printer` : Terminate the printer daemon and disable printing
- `Clean printer` : Remove any temporary, data, and control files that cannot be printed.
- `status [printer]` : Display the status of a printer
- `start printer` : Enable printing and start daemon
- `restart printer` : Start new printer daemon

For all these commands, printer is the name of the printer. All the commands except status can use the keyword `all` to perform a command on all the printers. The command `status` without any arguments displays the status of all the printers.

The following sequence of commands fixes almost every printing program:

```
/etc/lpc abort printer
/etc/lpc clean printer
/etc/lpc start printer
```

CREATING HARDWARE DEVICES

All the hardware devices are located in the /dev directory. Inside this directory is a Bourne shell program called MAKEDEV. At the top of the MAKEDEV file is a list of all the devices that can be made. For example, MAKEDEV contains the comment:

```
sd*     SCSI disks
```

To make a /dev file for the SCSI device, the argument "sd" must be supplied to the MAKEDEV program:

```
MAKEDEV sd
```

Before a hardware device is set up, the device must be made with MAKEDEV. Disk devices are a special case; in addition to creating the device, a partition must be formatted.

File System

Most system-management responsibilities involve file-system maintenance. Some of these responsibilities include:

1. Creating disk partitions
2. Monitoring disk usage
3. Implementing disk quotas
4. Fixing corrupt file partitions

CREATING DISK PARTITIONS

Creating a disk partition involves several steps. The first step is to look at the file /etc/disktab and find out the hardware device name of the disk you wish to partition. The second step is actually to create the partition with newfs. The third step is to assign a directory name to the partition.

Running newfs

The newsfs command creates a disk into the appropriate partitions. This command should be run only once for each disk partition. Running newfs destroys all the information in the partition of the disk.

The format of the newfs command is:

```
newfs [options] device
```

For a complete list of options and more information about the newfs command, please refer to the online manual.

Running newfs creates a directory called lost+found in every partition. All partitions must have this directory—any file that cannot be properly restored after a disk corruption is placed in this directory.

ASSIGNING A NAME TO A PARTITION

The file /etc/fstab (File System TABle) is a list of disk partitions and their names. This file contains:

1. Hardware device
2. Full path of the directory
3. Type: 4.3(local), 4.2(old version of local access), nfs(networked), or swap
4. Options: readonly, disk quotas
5. Frequency of dumps
6. Pass number for /etc/fsck

For example:

```
/dev/hd0f /usr 4.3 rw 7 1
```

Each entry associates a hardware partition with a partition name. This example allows read and write access; this access may be limited by file and directory permission modes.

An "empty" directory by this partition name ("usr") must be made in the root directory.

The number 7 in the previous example tells the system that this partition should be dumped to tape once every 7 days. If /etc/dump is not performed on this partition within 7 days of the previous dump, an electronic mail message is sent to root—notifying the system manager that the dump was not performed.

Each pass of /etc/fsck checks a different partition on a disk. The disks may be checked concurrently. The root directory having a pass number of zero is checked first. The second and subsequent passes checks one partition on each disk concurrently—starting with pass number one.

CHECKING FILE-SYSTEM CONSISTENCY

The program /etc/fsck checks for file-system consistency. This program is run every time the system is booted. All Unix systems have the command:

```
/etc/fsck -p
```

in the /etc/rc.boot file. The "-p" option tells fsck to check every file listed in /etc/fstab and to check the partitions in the order given. This option also tells fsck to attempt automatically to fix disk corruption problems. The fsck command should only be used when the system is in single-user mode because the file system should not change while the program is running.

MONITORING DISK USAGE

The df command shows the disk usage in all the partitions:

```
Filesystem    kbytes    used    avail capacity    Mounted on

/dev/hd0a    149364    108688    25739    81%        /
/dev/hd0b    86222     70482     7117     91%        /usr
```

When a file system becomes 100-percent full, no more information can be written to it. Depending on the activity of a disk partition, it should be kept under 90 to 98 percent full.

CREATING MAILING ALIASES

Mailing aliases are listed in the file /usr/lib/aliases. For example, the alias:

```
system:kay,jw@anotherhost
```

sends all mail addressed to system to kay and also sends the message to jw at computer font.

After editing the /usr/lib/aliases file, update the sendmail files with the command:

```
sendmail -bz
```

If a mailing list is run by some local user, this user can control additions and deletions to the list by having an include entry in /usr/lib/aliases. For example:

```
thelistname: :include:/usr/users/theuser/aliasfile
```

This file, /usr/users/theuser/aliasfile, is just a list of e-mail addresses of names on the list. For example:

```
jw@anotherhost
```

People are added and deleted by editing the file called **aliasfile**. The sendmail command does not need to be run when adding or deleting users in this manner.

SUMMARY

This chapter described some of the necessary topics to manage a Unix system. These functions included shutting down the system, adding new users, backups of the file system, printing, and mail aliases.

INDEX